HISTORY OF HANTS & DORSET MOTOR SERVICES LTD

for my godson
Trevor Brackston

HISTORY
OF HANTS & DORSET
MOTOR SERVICES LTD

COLIN MORRIS

David & Charles : Newton Abbot

0 7153 6051 5

The information in this book represents the position at 1 March 1973

Set in 11/13pt Garamond
and printed in Great Britain
by Latimer Trend & Company Ltd
for David & Charles (Holdings) Ltd
South Devon House Newton Abbot Devon

CONTENTS

LIST OF ILLUSTRATIONS

JACKET

Stowaways to Southampton; a Leyland G5 leaving Winchester in 1921 with several passengers in unorthodox places

LINE

MAPS

FOREWORD

When asked by the author, whom I have known since his college days, to write the foreword for this most fascinating story of the Hants & Dorset company, I gladly agreed—chiefly because I felt that there are many people who would wish to share with me the pleasure of reading about the lives and times of people who have given devoted public service and left their indelible mark upon the history of transport.

The narrative of this book, which contains many episodes and anecdotes, will enhance the reader's pleasure when he travels by 'Hants & Dorset' through the countryside of the lovely counties from which the company takes its name, on a holiday tour along roads that once witnessed the intrepid Mr Graham chauffeuring some of the nobility of Europe, or to the Continent—as foreseen by those who drew up the company's articles of association in 1916. There is much to stimulate the interest of newcomers to an industry presently undergoing tremendous change, yet which had its real beginnings in the period following the momentous years 1914–18, when men who had been disciplined by war, met the challenge of a new mode of transport and applied their own special skills to it.

My own 45 years service with the company began in the turbulent twenties, at the height of Hants & Dorset's struggle for supremacy over its many rivals. The epoch-making Road Traffic Act, 1930, terminated this period of fierce competition, but the detailed survey of routes, requested by the Traffic Commissioners, was—in many cases—only accomplished after consulting the crews who operated them. Thereafter, road service licensing became more and more specialised, until legal experts were called in for advocacy in many of the more complex and contentious claims for the trading advantages secured by the new legislation.

Hants & Dorset is now responsible for the operation of over 850 public service vehicles, yet all was built upon the assiduity of characters who live again in this book: my task brought me into very close contact with these pioneers and I am delighted to be able to pay tribute to them here.

Christchurch,
1972

HAROLD F. J. STEVENS
CHIEF LICENSING OFFICER
H & D M S

CHAPTER ONE

W. W. GRAHAM AND W. F. FRENCH

THE FAMILY GRAHAM

FRANCIS GRAHAM was a Lowland Scot. He came south from Lanarkshire in the first half of the nineteenth century and set up home in a cottage between Holdenhurst village and Hurn. Soon, he had acquired a horse and carriage and was offering transportation between Christchurch and Hurn Court.

At the time of his arrival, large areas of Poole Heath lay fallow and both east and west of Bourne valley, the gorse and pine trees crowded like spectators at the head of the tall sand-cliffs. Beneath, a stretch of unspoiled golden sand reached away to Hengistbury Head and Poole Harbour and at intervals, the cliffs were riven with those strange overgrown canyons known as 'the chines'. These old water courses provided an easy access to the hinterland and, for the most part, supported a luxuriant growth of low trees and bushes. For centuries they had proven a clandestine means of entry for contraband and undesirable persons alike.

In a spirit of adventure, Francis Graham decided to throw in his lot with the smugglers and provide them with a means of transport. He stepped up the efficiency of the operation by bringing a horse-drawn waggon on to the beach. In the small hours, this vehicle repeatedly crossed the heath and Stour Ford loaded with ankers of good Dutch brandy—a commercial transport undertaking which was to prove far more lucrative than the occasional day-time fare. Just what proportion of his income was culled in this fashion remains obscure, but it undoubtedly contributed to the early ownership of several more horses and carriages.

As the spread of the new seaside resort of Bournemouth made secret activities difficult on the one hand, it suggested with the other an increasing passenger traffic. Whilst his children were still young, Graham left Hurn and moved into a new house behind the West Cliff. At first, he went into business as a seedsman, but a cobbled yard and mews quickly took shape alongside his premises. He was certainly one of the earliest citizens of the resort, for Bournemouth in 1856 was described by a visitor as: '. . . one row of villas facing a wood, a couple of Hotels, Sydenham's Library on the beach—and the Bourne Stream trickling over the sand into the sea'.

Although the Lower Gardens were being planned, only a wooden bridge crossed the stream where The Square now stands: the first marshalling area for public vehicles was upon the semicircle of sand where the stream crossed the beach. A barouche owned by Francis Graham was one of the first carriages to vie for custom at this stand—carrying the passengers but a short distance to the hotels.

Bournemouth was not yet served by a railway. Travellers from the West Country alighted at Poole Station—later known as Hamworthy—and hailed a carriage to convey them into the town: often this was Graham's. From London and Southampton, the journey was far more complicated: the London & South Western Railway Company's line between Southampton and Dorchester had been designed to serve Brockenhurst, Ringwood and Wimborne—and swung around to the north of Bournemouth in a wide arc. Not surprisingly, it was dubbed the Watersnake or 'Castleman's Corkscrew'—a reference to the chief petitioner for the line. Initially, the nearest railway station to Bournemouth and Christchurch for passengers from the east was Christchurch Road Station, some eleven miles from the centre of the resort.

Sensing where the main source of revenue lay, Francis Graham now abandoned Hamworthy Station and—in competition with several others—began meeting the trains at Christchurch Road. Bournemouth-bound passengers quickly took advantage of this and the LSWR, taking note of their increasing number, laid belated plans to serve the town. A branch line was extended from Ringwood to Christchurch—but through passengers were required to change trains, which led to lengthy delays. Many continued to alight at Christchurch Road—which now became Holmsley Station. This served to produce yet more passengers for Graham and his rivals, for they were now able to collect them from both stations. In 1870, the Ringwood and Christchurch line was extended to Bournemouth itself—on to a site to the east of Holdenhurst Road, but this journey still involved an incredibly roundabout route and there were still very many who preferred to leave the trains at Holmsley.

Charles Graham, the elder of the sons, had been helping his father with this work for some little time, when a bizarre incident left him in sole charge. It would seem that Francis had not entirely mended his ways, for his great grand-daughter, Mrs Lory Hawker relates—with just a trace of delight: 'Great grandfather Francis became involved in a scuffle of some sort. He was probably doing a spot of smuggling again. Anyhow, he got a sword wound in the leg and this became infected. It eventually killed him.'

His father having become almost certainly the first and last citizen of Bournemouth to die by the sword, Charles Graham found himself in possession of the business. Whilst maintaining the station service, he began to develop the private-hire section with brakes and landaus. He had married a young lady from Poole, named Charlotte Wells and over the years they were blessed with three sons and a daughter.

In 1880, the coaches of Thomas Elliott—the founder of Royal Blue—appeared on the road to Holmsley. Contrary to popular belief, he did not pioneer the link between the station and the town. It had existed for many years. What he did introduce were new standards of efficiency and reliability. A thorough professional, he met the trains with several coaches and, at the Bournemouth end, drummed up support for the route from the clientele of the hotels. His popularity increased and he eventually made the route his own.

Charles Graham withdrew from what had become an uneven contest and concentrated solely upon the operation of small and medium-sized carriages from his West Cliff Mews in St Michael's

Road. However, his ambition did not match Tom Elliott's, for whilst Elliott's 'Royal Blue' went from strength to strength, by comparison Graham's stables remained an exceedingly modest affair.

The youngest son, William Wells Graham—known within the family circle as Dick—was born in 1878. He left school at the age of twelve and began work as a junior clerk in the office of the mayor at Richmond Chambers. So far, he had shown rather more interest in the personal comfort of his father's horses than the revenue which their labour secured. In the evenings, as William Graham helped to rub them down, there formed the opinion which was to play its part in later events: 'A horse was a lovable creature. To make him work hard and then sell him when he became too old, was most unkind. If he were to have horses of his own, he'd prefer that they'd lead lives of leisure. He'd make his money some other way.'

The young William Graham was no mean athlete. At 14 years, he joined the newly founded Bournemouth Swallows Football Club, a forerunner of Bournemouth & Boscombe Athletic. At the same time, he learned to play hockey—and was still turning out for the Bournemouth Sports Club thirty years on, at about which time he was to become proficient upon the golf course. Later, he was to take an interest in sailing, a sport which was to prove a major pastime in his mature years.

Meanwhile, with half an eye upon the expanding property market, his father arranged for him to be trained as an estate agent. This was to prove a short-lived occupation: the youngster soon realised that a totally chair-bound life was not for him and began to search for an out-door job of the kind which had served father and grandfather so well. Following an interview with Captain Masters of the paddle steamer *Monarch*, he entered upon a seasonal career as a steward. This vessel, owned by Cosens & Co of Weymouth, plied between Bournemouth, Swanage, Poole, Weymouth and the Isle of Wight. More often than not William Graham and his fellow crew members slept aboard the steamer.

It was becoming fashionable to spend Christmas in Bournemouth. The demand for transport grew accordingly and Charles

Graham's business began to flourish upon a year-round basis. William's months ashore made him available to help. Predictably, despite his concern for the finer ethical points, he eventually joined his father full-time. By 1900, there were ten horses and a like number of carriages available at the West Cliff Mews. The landau was most often employed during the winter months: in the summer it was the turn of the brakes and chars-à-banc. These were licensed by the Horse Committee of Bournemouth Corporation as Class 'A' vehicles with permission to operate tours from The Square between the hours of 10 and 11 in the morning and 2 and 3 in the afternoon. During the holiday season, tours to the New Forest were so popular that demand often exceeded available vehicles and many were disappointed. The fortunate left in convoy with carriages owned by Thomas Elliott, Futcher & Co, Mark Bryant and several others, amused by the continual banter of the drivers until the distances increased and the competitors' facetious replies faded on the wind.

Tours which left in the morning sometimes went as far as Lyndhurst and Rufus Stone, returning by way of Burley and some of the loveliest scenery in the forest. In the event of a late-evening return, brass paraffin lamps were lit, but drivers were under instructions to reach the gas-lit streets of the town before nightfall if at all possible. On warm summer evenings, a long queue of carriages would await their turn to cross the narrow Iford bridge; the steam from the horses rising in clouds above the waters of the Stour.

In increasing numbers, tiller-steered motor cars and motorised bicycles began to join this traditional traffic jam. Periodically, such a vehicle would backfire as the driver decelerated, causing the horses to start, swerve and sometimes damage themselves upon the shafts or against other vehicles. On one occasion, whilst standing outside the Bell Hotel at Brook, a horse was pushed to its knees as a motor car collided with the rear of the carriage. Such incidents strengthened William Graham's resolve to dispense with horses and become a mechanised operator, but his father became more firmly entrenched and resisted the call for modernisation. 'Those motors will be the death of you, my boy,' he pronounced darkly—and continued to operate horse-drawn vehicles until the beginning of World War I.

In 1903, William Graham purchased his first motor car: a tiller-steered Wolseley with transverse engine and leather belt transmission. At the same time, he became one of the founder members of the Bournemouth Automobile Association. That year marked the beginning of the motor car boom in the town. Bournemouth had not introduced a speed limit and left the matter of regulation to the gentlemanly instincts of its new motorists. Elsewhere, unfortunate police forces were obliged to attempt the enforcement of limits imposed by the local authorities. Christchurch, Southampton town and county councils introduced 10mph limits within built-up areas and set the scene for a war of nerves between motorists and policemen which went to incredible lengths. Maps went on sale, advising that police 'ambuscades' could be expected at Iford (though clearly not on the bridge), Hinton Admiral, Brockenhurst, the Avenue in Southampton, etc, and disclosing the exact locality. Policemen dressed as road menders, hay-makers or tramps popped out from behind bushes, waving handkerchiefs and consulting stop-watches. Motorists leaped from their cars and attempted to photograph the disguised officers, who promptly ran off, lest they be recognised. Furthermore, their task was extremely difficult, for it was not until the end of 1903 that cars bore number plates. Such was the changing world in which William Graham learned his new trade. It is clear that, at this stage, nothing was further from his mind than the running of omnibuses.

BOURNEMOUTH'S EARLY BUSES

Stage carriage services in Bournemouth stemmed from the original rail-head routes—Hamworthy and Holmsley. From 1866, a horse bus ran between the new station at Westbourne and The Square and—four years later—Bournemouth East. There were several small fleets in action during the next thirty years, but most withdrew to concentrate upon the tourist trade. At the close of

Page 17 *(above)* William Wells Graham, OBE, FIMT; *(right)* The Poole Hill premises of W. W. Graham & Co, around which the new bus company was built

Visitor's car at the West Cliff Mews: former groom William Cox at right

Page 18 Silver Fleet charabancs: Bournemouth & District's first vehicles were aluminium painted Straker Squires. Here, one is about to depart from Bournemouth with a full load of wounded soldiers in September 1916

'Tickets for Mr. Harvey's Motor Boats can be obtained from the conductress.' An AEC charabanc—with Daimler radiator—on the Poole to Sandbanks stage carriage service

the century, the three main companies licensed to operate within the borough were:

Messrs. Mate & Peter's 'Bournemouth, Boscombe & Westbourne Omnibus Company Ltd'
Messrs. Horsey & Roll's 'General Penny Omnibus Company Ltd'
Messrs. Welsman & Hinton's 'Boscombe Park, Pokesdown & Southbourne Omnibus Syndicate Ltd', which became the 'Southbourne, Boscombe & Bournemouth Omnibus Company Ltd' in January 1900

All three fleets included double-decked buses drawn by two or three horses abreast.

In September 1899, their timetables were co-ordinated and a full-time omnibus timekeeper was appointed to see that this was observed. That month, the first MMC wagonette of the Canford Cliffs Motor Omnibus Company took to the streets, narrowly beating Edgar Collett's of Boscombe, to be joined later by two others. By 1901, John Norman and Francis Bell had joined the pioneers, the latter joining forces with a Mr Pickford to form Bournemouth Motors Ltd. This early flurry of activity was at its height the following spring, with Bournemouth Motors holding licences for nine, E. W. Collett and J. S. Norman two apiece and the Canford Cliffs company, three. All the wagonettes had been built by the Motor Manufacturing Company of Coventry.

Bournemouth Corporation's tramcars began running in July 1902 and, following an arrangement with Poole Corporation, were soon operating right through to Poole Railway Station. This effectively erased the horse buses and all save one of the motorised operators—the Canford Cliffs company surviving because the larger part of its route lay without the borough. F. J. Bell made an unsuccessful attempt to gain licences in Southampton and then left for London, where he operated similar vehicles at Putney with a degree of success, until he failed to master heavier opposition. In 1903, all save the Canford Cliffs company exchanged their 'B' licences (for stage carriage work) for Group 'A' and operated tours.

W. W. GRAHAM & COMPANY

The demand was for garage space. Visitors and residents alike were forbidden to leave their cars unattended on the street, because a locking switch was not yet in general use. Overnight parking was unheard of: if one could offer accommodation for the cars and chauffeurs of the wealthy visitors, there was money to be made. William Graham decided that his moment had arrived. He succeeded in talking his father into granting him some land adjacent to his livery stables. Mr and Mrs William Graham then pooled their savings, founded W. W. Graham & Company and erected a garage. This, a rather modest affair, they named the West Cliff Garage and opened for business in 1905.

Among those who transferred some of their attentions from Charles Graham's business was a former groom, William Cox. Initially he found the transition from horse to motor car a little difficult—a groom's conditioned reflex took charge each time he polished a car. He would rub a little, then blow—in order to dispel the dust from the 'horsehair'. Yet Cox was destined to outlast all the original members of the business—going on to the payroll of Hants & Dorset and serving under four different general managers in one capacity or another.

Inevitably, as the popularity of Bournemouth increased, so too did the demand for transport, and W. W. Graham & Co, were to prove equal to the challenge. In 1911, premises upon Poole Hill were acquired. These had previously served as stables and were still equipped with hay loft and hoist. (This building is at present the office of Charlie's Cars, a business founded by another local pioneer, Charles J. Pounds, upon an earlier concern run by his father Shadrach.) From here, Wolseley Landaulettes and Arrol-Johnston touring cars were offered for hire. Graham became an agent for Hampton and—more important—the New Arrol-Johnston Car Company Ltd. This Paisley manufacturer enjoyed a period of popularity after winning the Tourist Trophy race in 1905. Arrol-Johnston cars were always well represented in

Graham's pre-World War I fleet and he was responsible for the sale of many 11·9hp models. A large six-cylinder model was to become his first char-à-banc in 1912. This—a nine seater—conveyed private parties from Graham's garages and was thus able to operate without the usual Horse Committee licence. (The latter had extended their interest to motorised vehicles—an arrangement which continued until the committee was suitably renamed in the twenties.)

Further expansion involved the acquisition of the Savoy Garage, attached to the hotel of that name in nearby West Cliff Road. This became Mrs Lory Graham's responsibility and she proceeded to build up a reputation for efficiency and courtesy which attracted custom from the notable guests of the Savoy Hotel. The lock-ups became the regular winter quarters for the vehicles and chauffeurs of the Duke of Connaught. His Grace then proved happy to recommend the Grahams to the Imperial Russian Ambassador to the Court of St James—and William Graham was thereafter engaged as his personal driver during his visits to Bournemouth.

Graham's company was awarded the final accolade during the last great Imperial get-together before the onset of World War I. Kaiser Wilhelm II and his party, which included his nephew the Crown Prince of Bavaria and Dr Krupp von Bohlen und Halbach, arrived for Cowes Week and stayed at Highcliffe Castle to the east of Bournemouth. Graham was commissioned by Ludwig, the Crown Prince, to take his party on a tour of Devon and Cornwall.

WALTER FLEXMAN FRENCH

As the war clouds were gathering over Europe, a councillor for the London Borough of Wandsworth arrived for a holiday in Bournemouth and placed his car in the Grahams' care. Although not known in international circles, this visitor was to prove their most important customer. The small silver-haired man was one of the most famous of commercial motor pioneers—Walter Flexman French. A founder member of the Society of Motor

Engineers, he had commenced his career in 1881 as a manufacturer of bicycles at Bedford Hill, Balham. Following the repeal of the 'Red Flag Act' in 1896, he had begun to take a serious interest in motor cars and three years later was operating a pair of Daimler wagonettes on stage carriage services between Putney and Piccadilly, later abandoning the route (which was taken up by Bournemouth's own F. J. Bell) and running between Streatham and Balham.

He had retired from the cycle business in 1903 and the following year become manager and engineer for the Sussex Motor Road Car Company Ltd, then a struggling concern operating steam buses. These he replaced with new Milnes Daimler vehicles, designing the double-decked bodies for several and supervising their construction. After the acquisition of the Worthing Motor Omnibus Company, he succeeded in pushing the operating area eastwards to Brighton and westward to Portsmouth—and so very nearly to Southampton (see Chapter Five).

By 1909 he had returned to London and launched French's Ltd (Motor Jobmasters), hiring out 40hp Ryknield wagons for retail delivery work. He attracted business by guaranteeing any firm hiring one or more of his wagons for a six-month period and losing on the transaction, a complete refund of their losses. This secured the custom of the Anglo-American Oil Company and many others—and no one asked for a refund. Acting as London manager for the manufacturers, he was also responsible for the sale of several Ryknield omnibuses to the Brussels municipal authority.

When he first met William Graham, Flexman French was already a leading figure in Maidstone & District Motor Services and the Aldershot & District Traction Company, with influential friends in British Automobile Traction—a British Electric Traction Company subsidiary. Soon he became a friend of the family and a business confidant. Whilst being entertained at St Michael's Road he pointedly remarked upon the absence of an inter-urban omnibus service in the area, of the type working elsewhere. Initially Graham was sceptical, recalling the example of the Isle of Wight Express Motor Syndicate, whose double-decker bus services across the island had folded some years before. But gradually he became convinced that his business and the goodwill which had been built up over the years, could form the nucleus for a new omnibus company. French emphasised that the existing car-hire business could be operated side by side with the stage carriage work and would most likely be enhanced by it.

With the project now accepted and agreed in principle, Walter Flexman French contacted his friend and colleague Sidney Garcke of BAT. The weight of the British Electric Traction Company was thus enlisted and the serious business of costing out began. A new company was to be formed which would become an integral part of a planned series of services linking the South Coast with London.

CHAPTER TWO

BOURNEMOUTH & DISTRICT MOTOR SERVICES LTD

THE SILVER FLEET

BOURNEMOUTH & DISTRICT MOTOR SERVICES LTD was registered as a private company on 17 March 1916, with a nominal capital of £30,000. Walter Flexman French was elected chairman, Sidney Garcke represented the interest of the British Electric Traction Company and William Wells Graham became at once co-director and general manager. Among the twenty-eight objects listed in the company's articles of association are the following:

a. To adopt and carry into effect, either with or without modification, an agreement dated 29 February 1916, made between James McMeekin and Walter F. French.

b. To purchase, lease, establish or otherwise acquire any tramway or light railway, or any trolley vehicle (being any mechanically propelled vehicle adapted for use upon roads and moved by electric power transmitted thereto from some external source), motor or other omnibus, ship, boat, aeroplane or airship, or motor or other cab undertakings in the United Kingdom or elsewhere, and to construct any motor omnibuses, motor or other cabs, trolley or other vehicles (whether earth, air or waterborne), tramways or light railways, and to equip, maintain and work, either by horses or steam or electricity or gas or oil engine, or wire rope or by electrical power, or by any mechanical power whatsoever, all tramways, light railways, trolley vehicle, motor or other omnibus, ship, boat, aeroplane or airship, or motor or other cab undertaking, belonging to or leased to the company or over which the company may possess a right to run and work.

On 1 May 1916, some few weeks after the registration, Sidney Garcke handed over his interest to BET colleague James Spagnoletti and retired from the board. Despite this, his family's influence was to remain a further twenty years, during which period over 130 bus bodies built by the Brush Electrical Engineering Company were to be purchased—a company managed and chaired for many years by his father, Emile Garcke.

Although the registered office of the new company was at first located in the Wilts & Dorset Bank Chambers (a noteworthy address in the light of events some fifty years later!), at Bournemouth, throughout the first year the wages were sent weekly from London.

Immediately, the directors found the utmost difficulty in obtaining suitable vehicles for public service. All new three- and four-ton chassis were earmarked for military service and it was only the influence of BAT which secured four chassis from Straker Squire Industrial Motors of Blackfriars, being part of an order diverted from Maidstone & District Motor Services Ltd. These were sent to Poole, where char-à-banc bodies were fitted and painted in the aluminium livery of 'The Silver Fleet'—an unofficial trading name for the company's early touring chars-à-banc. At Mrs Graham's suggestion, each bore an individual name upon the rear panelling and the original four became respectively, *The Silver King*, *The Silver Queen*, *The Silver Prince* and *The Silver Princess*. In order to give the impression that the fleet was larger than it was in fact, only even numbers were used—a device first employed by Lyons of 'Corner House' fame (with odd numbers only) for their fleet of delivery vans. The company was to pursue this even-numbers-only policy until 1939.

The chars-à-banc were intended to give local employees experience in the operation of large vehicles and were employed upon tours under Class 'A' licences issued by the Horse Committee of Bournemouth Corporation—two on 15 May and the remainder on 19 June 1916. That spring, the council had turned down a plea that women might be permitted to drive, but granted instead permission for them to conduct motor chars-à-banc. The minimum age for conductors had been lowered to sixteen years at the turn of the century, so the time was ripe for a teen-age young lady who, acting upon a patriotic impulse, offered her services. Thus Driver Lee and his conductress, Miss Dennett, became the first mixed crew of a company omnibus. Miss Dennett later became Mrs J. T. G. Elliott, wife of the managing director of Royal Blue Automobile Services Ltd.

THE 'PAPER' FLEET

The serious business of acquiring stage carriage licences began in May 1916, with a letter from William Graham to the chairman of the Horse Committee. A copy is proudly preserved by Hants & Dorset Motor Services Ltd and reads:

BOURNEMOUTH & DISTRICT MOTOR SERVICES LTD.
W. W. GRAHAM & CO.

West Cliff Garage,
St. Michael's Road,
BOURNEMOUTH.

The Chairman & Members of
The Horse Committee,
Borough of Bournemouth.

13 May 1916.

Gentlemen,

We beg to make application for omnibus licences, and an arranged stopping place for the purpose of opening a regular service of Motor Omnibuses.

It is our wish to start a service commencing with:—

Lymington, via Iford, Christchurch, Highcliffe, Barton, Mudeford, Milton &c.,
and later on to:—

Ringwood via Ferndown
Wimborne „ Kinson & Canford
Southampton via Iford, Christchurch & Lyndhurst, and any other routes which may from time to time be found necessary.

To carry this plan out we would suggest that you allot us a stopping place near the centre of the town, from which we could start a continuous and regular service. It could be arranged that the cars were there only a few minutes, and to stop any possibility of competition with the Corporation Trams we would make our fares, whilst on the tram routes, at least 2d. more than the Tram Fares.

The writer has recently visited Reading, Maidenhead, Worthing, Brighton and several other towns where Bus services are running, and has found in every case that they are looked upon as an acquisition and help to the welfare of their town, being of a great assistance to visitors and bringing a large number of County residents into their towns every week for shopping, Concerts, Amusements &c. &c.

Needless to say, our cars will be of the latest and best type, and with your kind assistance will, we feel sure, be looked upon as an improvement and credit to the Borough.

The writer, who is General Manager, and a Director of the Company, will arrange to be at home on the day of your next meeting, and if there are any points you may wish to discuss a 'phone message will cause him to wait on you immediately.

Trusting these proposals will meet with your favourable consideration and approval.

We remain,

Yours respectfully,

The Bournemouth & District
Motor Services Ltd.

W. W. Graham
General Manager.

Although mildly puzzled, the chairman did not telephone, but chose to reply in writing. The tone of the letter from Herbert Ashling, the Town Clerk, may well have surprised Graham, particularly since the two were not averse to an occasional pheasant-shoot together. But it can hardly have had the same effect upon such a seasoned campaigner as Walter Flexman French.

County Borough of Bournemouth

Town Clerks Office
Bournemouth

TC/W 18th May 1916

Dear Sirs,

My Committee have had before them your letter of the 13th instant and have instructed me to write you for further details of your suggestions.

They would like to know, having regard to the fact chars-à-banc are licenced in this Town under class A (with which you are doubtless familiar) why your purpose would not be served by applying for licences under this class.

The Committee note your suggestion of making the fares 2d. beyond the present Tramway fares. Are they to understand that this means that you propose to take up and set down passengers along the tramway routes?

The Committee would be very glad if you would show them any statistics or other facts tending to prove that such a service as you propose is required in the Borough, particularly seeing that a large number of chars-à-banc are already licenced.

Yours Faithfully,

H. Ashling

Town Clerk

The truth of the matter was that unbeknown to Graham, the application was ill-timed. Only one week prior to this the Corporation had received notification of the Local Government (Emergency Provisions) Bill to which the County Councils Association had successfully caused the following to be added:

1. Notwithstanding anything in any statute it shall not be lawful after the passing of this Act for any omnibus to ply for hire on, or use, any route which has not been regularly used by omnibuses plying for hire within twelve months prior to the first day of March, nineteen hundred and sixteen, except with the consent of the highway authority, or, if more than one, every highway along which the route runs, which consent may be given on such conditions as the highway authority may consider fit, or, if such consent is unreasonably refused, without the consent of the Local Government Board: and if any person drives an omnibus or allows an omnibus to be driven along any route in contravention of this provision, he shall, on summary conviction be liable to a fine not exceeding five pounds and to a further penalty not exceeding forty shillings for every mile travelled by every omnibus in contravention of the provisions of this section, all penalties recoverable under this section to be paid into the funds of the highway authority concerned: Provided that nothing in this section shall apply where a route is altered in consequence of the temporary diversion of traffic on account of the breaking up of any road or in pursuance of the direction of any police authority or other

directions lawfully given: Provided also that nothing in this section shall apply to any omnibus plying for hire on any route in any case where the Admiralty, Army Council, or Minister of Munitions are of the opinion that an omnibus service is necessary for and is to be used solely by munition workers or other persons engaged on Government War Service.
2. This section shall not be deemed to detract from any existing powers of highway authorities in regard to omnibuses.
3. For the purposes of this section the expression "omnibuses" includes every omnibus, char-à-banc, wagonette, brake, stage coach, or other carriage plying for hire or used to carry passengers at separate fares.

The government was anxious that the roads, and particularly those in the south of England, should not be submitted to further wear than necessary. The full impact of the motorisation of military transport was beginning to be felt on the roads to the south coast ports, on Salisbury Plain, at Aldershot and in the New Forest. It was to be left to the discretion of the local highway authority to decide which roads required such protection.

If Bournemouth & District's application had been submitted but one month earlier it is highly likely that the projected services would have been sanctioned within a matter of weeks. In the event, the negotiations fizzled and a full three years elapsed before the necessary licences were granted. Letters passed between Balham, West Cliff Garage and the Town Clerk's Office throughout the summer of 1916, before the company at last decided to withdraw and examine its position.

Graham to Town Clerk:

I am under the impression that licences held under Class "A" only allow the holder to pick up between 10 & 11 a.m. and 2 & 3 p.m., and are therefore not suitable for omnibus routes. My Company wish to prevent competition with the trams and the suggested charge of 2d in excess of the tramfares was made that your Committee might have ground for discussion.

Town Clerk to Graham:

Your impression with regard to licences held under Class "A" is incorrect. I enclose a copy of the omnibus Bylaws for your perusal.

W. F. French to William Graham:

> I do not know the extent of the Borough, but I believe it only extends as far as Pokesdown. Competition with the Trams is not the aim. (true, the boundary was at Pokesdown, but the Corporation Tramway ran on into Christchurch. The Chairman had not done his homework on this point.) Suggest a minimum fare of 3d over the tram. Tell the clerk that a char-à-banc picks up at one well-defined spot and charges return fares only and on a much heavier scale than buses. The country people will come into the town to shop. A bus leaving the country villages every hour or so is of inestimable value as in the case of Maidstone and Brighton. The towns offering the greatest travelling facilities are those enjoying the greatest progress. Many thousands who do not now come into Bournemouth more than twice a year would come weekly. The Company is willing to offer these facilities.

To the conservative councillors of the Borough this last point may well have spelled anathema. True, several were business men, but all were concerned with the preservation of that character which is peculiarly Bournemouth's and did not, in any sense wish to transform the resort into a market town. Graham to Town Clerk—(with commendable optimism):

> I am willing to leave the selection of a stopping place to your Committee. Whilst pointing out that my Company do not wish to compete with the Trams, neither do they wish to compete with the existing charabancs.

(The use of the word 'charabancs' is noteworthy, since it was about this time that the French term 'chars-à-banc' was replaced in official literature with the anglicised version, 'charabancs'—pronounced '*sharrabangs*'.)

Anxious to secure the route to Lymington, the company were concurrently negotiating with the authorities to the east of the borough. From this quarter, their overtures were greeted more favourably: the following being a typical reply:

> The Town Clerk, Lymington. 3 July
>
> The Town Council will probably be pleased to offer facilities, but before making any definite promise, the Highways Committee would like to hear more about your proposals. The Committee are

concerned to know (a) if the citizens of Lymington will be able to return to the town after having visited Bournemouth, (b) what scale of fares is proposed, (c) what timetable is proposed. It would seem that you intend catering for the citizens of Bournemouth rather than those of Lymington and the intermediate villages.

Suitably encouraged, Graham made a strong appeal to the Town Clerk of Bournemouth, emphasising the following points: That:

1. The Christchurch and Lymington Councils and the Lymington Rural District Council are in favour of the scheme—in fact the District Council wish the Buses to Commence next month.

2. From a patriotic and War point of view, I must mention that the whole of the eligible staff of the Company (21 in number) have voluntarily enlisted.

3. Owners of private cars have had to stop using them and they now need means of getting into town. The Government having taken over the supply of petrol, have allotted the Company a supply sufficient for the next four months. It would prove a better service to the country if this were used on a regular bus service.

I trust the Committee will reconsider the matter. Bournemouth should not be left in the lurch. A large proportion of the general public who are not able to keep a car will benefit.

My Company wish to prevent competition with the trams.

Applying the pressure where the battle was going well, Graham next penned a note to the Town Clerk of Lymington:

We have not yet completed arrangements with Bournemouth Corporation. They are anxious to prevent competition with the trams. If they do not consent we shall take the question to higher authority. Your Rural District Council wish the service to start as soon as possible.

We are getting some fine bus bodies built and should lose no time in making a start.

I trust your council will consider the question favourably, as I feel sure that it would be of great mutual benefit to your town and district.

From Lymington came the reply which had been so eagerly sought. The town was to be the first to grant positive operating rights to the company:

HERBERT E. TIZARD,
TOWN CLERK.

Borough of Lymington.

SIGILLVM : BVRGI : DE : LYMINGTON

Town Hall,
Lymington.
9th August 1916

Dear Sir,

re proposed Motor Bus Service.

This matter is coming before my Town Council to-morrow (Thursday) when the Highways Committ will recommend that consent be given so far as this Borough is concerned.

Can you let me know before the Meeting at 11. a either by letter or by wire, whether you have al other necessary consents, and if yea, when the service is likely to commence.

I will write you again after to-morrow's Meeting

Yours faithfully
Herbert E. Tizard
Town Clerk

W. W. Graham Esq
Bournemouth & District Motor Services Ld.
West Cliff Garage
St. Michael's Road
Bournemouth

A welcome letter from Lymington Borough Council. Town Clerk Herbert Tizard was to prove a staunch supporter of the emergent company

> This matter is coming before . . . Council tomorrow . . . [10 August 1916] when the Highways Committee will recommend that consent be given so far as this Borough is concerned.

A breakthrough; yet almost three full years were to elapse before the company could capitalise upon it and those 'fine bus bodies' were actually built. For, in the first week of September, all doubt was dispelled. The company had failed to make any inroads upon the stand of the Horse and Tramways Committees. Bournemouth Corporation finally declared that they were not prepared to grant permission for the company to operate omnibuses in the town.

At a hastily convened meeting the directors discussed and rejected a suggestion that this set-back should be circumvented by moving the sphere of operations eastward to be centred upon Lymington. This would have involved an unacceptable dead mileage between the town and the garage in St Michael's Road, Bournemouth, and wasted large quantities of rationed fuel. Establishing a depot in Lymington would have involved the employment of a complete new set of personnel and nullified the original concept of a company which was to expand from the existing small-car business at West Cliff Garage.

Instead it was decided to maintain the fleet of charabancs for as long as circumstances would permit—whilst being prepared to introduce stage carriage operations at the earliest opportunity. Peace alone could retrieve the situation. Negotiations would be reopened with the Horse Committee when the prospects of an agreement seemed more favourable.

AN EXPLANATION

The emergency provisions had provided the local authority with the lever by which they were able to obstruct a potential competitor—but at this point it would be fair to examine the position of the Borough of Bournemouth. The council had behaved with the utmost propriety and there can be little doubt that the welfare of the town's citizens was uppermost in their minds. Once a municipal authority commits itself to the operation of passenger transport (or any other service, for that matter) it must be run in such a manner that it does not impose too large a burden upon the general rate. Indeed, under ideal circumstances, the service should be in a position to contribute toward the relief of the rates.

Yet, whilst Southampton Corporation Tramways, owning some seventy trams and serving a fairly static population, were able to operate at a profit, Bournemouth was not so fortunate. Then, as now, the town which fairly burst at the seams during the summer, entertained far fewer visitors throughout the rest of the year. To cope with the peak-period traffic, the corporation operated ninety-two trams. A large number of these lay idle during the winter months, failing to earn their keep, yet requiring continual mechanical repair, maintenance and cleaning. Under the circumstances, it was inevitable that the corporation tramways required a handsome subsidy from the rates.

In one respect, the corporation were hoist by their own petard. This august body had entered the passenger transport field to forestall the intention of the Poole & District Traction Company —a subsidiary of BET—to build and operate a tramway in the town. Now, in 1916, some of the councillors openly regretted the decision to do so.

If the Poole company had been permitted to construct their lines within the Borough, the off-peak loss would have become the annual headache of the British Electric Traction Group. Holidaymakers and citizens alike would have enjoyed a facility provided at no embarrassment to the corporation save that of municipal pride.

Here then, in the middle of a European War which imposed severe restrictions in man power and fuel, was a private company offering to provide a public service at a time when their own services were unable to break even. True, this company were offering to charge fares 3d in excess of the trams whilst operating within the Borough, but human nature had to be taken into account. Very many potential passengers, particularly those in

Page 35 (*above*) Sandbanks bus, 1912: The Canford Cliffs Motor Omnibus Company's Milnes Daimler wearing its open body for summer service; (*below*) Sandbanks bus, 1952: the prototype Hants & Dorset open-top body mounted on a Leyland TD4. Rejuvenated Bristol Ks fitted with these bodies worked the service for the next sixteen years

Page 36 (*above*) A Canford Cliffs Milnes Daimler, one of a pair which became the company's first saloon omnibuses

(*above*) A Morris 'One-ton' chaser. It chased, but seldom caught! (*below*) Successful chasing was achieved with acquired vehicles like this fine Thornycroft A1 Long, which became No 204 in the Hants & Dorset fleet

holiday mood, would have gladly paid the additional fares for the novelty of riding in a modern motor bus. As it was, with so many motormen and conductors having marched-off to war, the department were unable to maintain a regular service. Deprived of further revenue, the Tramways Committee would have been forced to ask the Treasurer to dig deeper into the pockets of the townfolk—and the very existence of the system would have been threatened from within. Other matters, such as the additional wear and tear upon the roads had been taken into account, but the corporation's main concern was to defray the expenses, protect the ratepayers of the Borough and—along with everyone else—pray for an end to the war.

One other factor should not be overlooked. Bournemouth Corporation had obtained powers to operate motor omnibuses in 1903 and the Tramways Department had placed a 3-ton Berna char-à-banc on service between April and September of 1906. It was used upon steeply-sloping Sea Road, Boscombe, between the Arcade and the Pier. Although only one-half mile in length, the haul up this hill had caused considerable wear upon engine, transmission and chassis and resulted in the withdrawal of the vehicle in May 1910. A replacement bus survived but one season and the venture had lost some £1,500. Four years later the department tried again. This time it was a little more adventurous and purchased two Tilling-Stevens open toppers and two Daimler single decks. The same route was resurrected and, for a brief period, operated efficiently, but the following spring, the Daimlers had been snapped up by the War Department.

Further vehicles had trials on other roads, but this time it was only the sharp decline in manpower because of the war, which left the department with but two omnibuses and two routes.

It was clear then, that the Tramways Department and Committee had briefly tasted the fruit of successful motorbus operation. Some members of the committee firmly believed that given peacetime conditions, a fleet of motor omnibuses, acting as feeders, could rescue the tram services. Furthermore, bearing in mind the extreme cost of track replacement—which took place upon average every seven years—together with the resultant disruption to other traffic, might it not be a good idea to replace the entire system with buses? Indeed, if these could be run at a profit, as it now seemed possible, then surely it was their duty to see that such revenue accrued to the corporation, rather than a private company.

Thus, within the Horse and Tramways Committees, there were two factions. One believed that the new company should be denied lest their profits were made at the expense of the struggling tramway system, whilst the other foresaw the possibility of a large-scale motorbus fleet owned and operated by the corporation in the peacetime which they felt was just around the corner. Although they held divergent views, the factions were not rivals. They both believed that it was in the interest of the ratepayers that Bournemouth & District Motor Services should change its name and go somewhere else.

In the event, the trams did go, the corporation did convert to motor buses and make a profit, the private company became public and changed its name and went to many other places—but the headquarters remained firmly entrenched at Bournemouth. In the long run then, both parties were to achieve their ambitions—but it was to be a very long run indeed before all these things came to pass.

WAR SERVICE

The managing director now devoted most of his time to voluntary service. In 1914 he had provided one of his small chars-à-banc for the transportation of wounded soldiers from Bournemouth's stations to the local hospitals. He and his fellow volunteers soon found that the charabanc was a most unsuitable vehicle for this work—the stretcher cases lying across the seats were in grave danger of being tumbled to the floor if the car stopped suddenly. Instead, two hire cars from the West Cliff Garage were converted into ambulances. There followed an assault upon the family's sofas and armchairs which provided cross supports for the stretchers. Within weeks several local owners had loaned cars for conversion and an Ambulance Corps had been formed. It was placed on call day or night when hospital trains were expected in the town.

Now, in 1916, the War Department formally recognised the unit and Lieutenant William Graham of the Motor Volunteer Transport became the officer commanding.

One of the more important innovations for which his corps was responsible was the Mobile X-Ray Unit. Under the guidance of Bournemouth doctors Bottomley, Malpas and Penrose, a rudimentary X-ray machine was installed in one of the original ambulances—with the khaki clad O.C., acting as personal assistant to the radiographer. They were thus able to relieve the pressure upon the hospitals and deliver the wounded with advance information upon the nature of their injuries. The batteries from the rest of the private hire fleet were packed into several ambulances to provide power for further mobile units. No protection was provided for the operators—the dangers of radiation being little known. One must presume that a fair amount of tissue damage was suffered by these pioneers during the two years the service was provided. The ambulances were maintained until after the end of hostilities and the Bournemouth hospitals had returned to a peace-time footing.

In recognition of his services in this field William Graham was made a Serving Brother of the Order of St John.

Tours with the Straker Squire charabancs continued to operate from The Square. An increasing number of recuperating soldiers —identified by their white shirts and red ties—began to occupy the available places. Despite the 'military' nature of this work, it was not the kind envisaged by the Emergency Provisions and the company began to encounter further difficulties. Petrol became more strictly rationed, the tours less regular and the War Department interested in acquiring the vehicles.

By 1917 a thoroughly frustrating situation had developed. At times the company had the four licences to operate, but insufficient petrol to take advantage of them. On other occasions they found enough petrol and custom to hire other vehicles, but could not obtain the extra licences. When fuel supplies were low they could not afford to let their existing licences lapse in case they proved difficult to recover.

These troubles aside, the War Department now requisitioned two of the charabancs. In an attempt to keep the others running the company examined the possibility of propulsion by town gas (the two remaining Tilling-Stevens omnibuses of the corporation were being operated in this fashion at this time), but this was thwarted by a further government move. A Gas Restriction Order came into force in January 1918, which made gas for motor vehicles subject to the same restrictions as petrol. It became necessary to obtain a Gas Permit from the Petrol Control Department of the Board of Trade—and this, it was explained, could only be granted for the purpose of stage carriage services. Despite the irony of the situation, the company could do little more than admit that they didn't operate any!

For a brief period the touring licences were retained by the stratagem of hiring other operators' vehicles—notably those of Mark Bryant's Executors—but at the least sign of a general increase of traffic, they naturally preferred to keep their vehicles. Much against his will, Graham was forced to reintroduce a pair of two-horse charabancs. Following the requisition of the two remaining Straker Squires, these horse-drawn vehicles—the property of W. W. Graham & Co—were the only rolling stock in the employ of Bournemouth & District Motor Services Ltd.

The War Department sent at least three of the Straker Squire charabancs to the Middle East: an ex-employee of the company, serving with the Army Service Corps in Mesopotamia, was placed in charge of the vehicles. Yet the licence records reveal that the legal ownership of all four remained with the company until 25 October 1920. It could well be that their eventual return was intended, but this was never implemented.

Two full years had elapsed since the foundation of the company, when at last a route was found which was not under the jurisdiction of Bournemouth Corporation, yet was within a very reasonable distance of St Michael's Road.

Under the terms of the Emergency Provisions, permission to open a new route in war-time was highly unlikely. The best hope lay in acquiring an existing business. On the road between County Gates and Sandbanks, just inside the Poole boundary, two small concerns had continued to struggle against the difficulties imposed by the times. They now seemed willing to sell. The company were about to embark upon their first stage carriage service—in Dorset.

CHAPTER THREE

THE CURTAIN RAISERS

THROUGHOUT WORLD WAR I, a group of Bournemouth townsfolk maintained a watch over Poole Bay in order to protect the area from the attentions of German surface raiders. This cliff-top patrol—a kind of maritime observer corps—was the meeting place for several of those who later played a leading part in the shaping of the post-war resort. It was upon such a Sunday-night patrol that William Graham first began the informal discussions which led to the acquisition of the stage carriage service between County Gates and Sandbanks. The two proprietors concerned were Eugene Poulain and the first of them all, the Canford Cliffs Motor Omnibus Company.

THE CANFORD CLIFFS MOTOR OMNIBUS COMPANY

Sandbanks is a club shaped peninsula guarding the entrance to Poole Harbour. At its base, the land above the sand cliffs is densely covered with the pine trees which once graced the western edge of Poole Heath. The woods are now studded with desirable properties, yet it seems that not one tree has been disturbed during their planning and construction. This much-admired area is Branksome Park and the *unique and commanding situation of the grounds adjacent to the sea front*, Canford Cliffs.

In the late nineteenth century, when only pine needles and heather covered the undulating sand, local estate agent and auctioneer Frank Holloway obtained permission to develop it, joined forces with C. R. Hutchings and formed the Canford

Cliffs Land Society. Progress was at first slow: one of the difficulties being the transportation of workmen from Poole and Bournemouth. Horse-drawn brakes were hired and one return journey was made each day from both towns. In 1898 the partners felt that an experiment with motor traction would be justified and that vacant seats might be offered to the public in order to defray running costs.

The 'Canford Cliffs Motor Omnibus Company' was formed in the summer of 1899 with an MMC wagonette, which commenced running from The Square, Bournemouth in September of that year. Both vehicle and Walter LeBreton, its driver, were awarded the very first Bournemouth licences for motor omnibus operation. The immediate success of the service led to the purchase of two more MMCs and pleased the Motor Manufacturing Company, who named the type 'the Canford' in subsequent literature. Although similar vehicles appeared within the Borough of Bournemouth, the lack of opposition on the section between County Gates and the Canford Estate Office during the early years, strengthened the position of the omnibus company.

When tramlines were laid in Bournemouth, the only effect was a brief suspension of licences to operate between County Gates and The Square. For those operating buses within the Borough the trams spelled ruin, but the Canford Cliffs MMC's eventually resumed service along the whole of the route and continued to do so for the next ten years. Nevertheless, they became increasingly difficult to maintain: more often than not, when spare parts did arrive they could not be made to fit the original and, to crown matters, by 1906 the Motor Manufacturing Company had been wound up.

When George Fox joined the company as a driver in March 1906, the two vehicles currently on the road required careful nursing. He recalled:

> They had flame-ignition engines, no water coolers and could only manage twelve miles per hour—downhill! Coming up Poole Hill out of Bournemouth was always a hit-or-miss affair: most occasions, I used to ask some passengers to get out and walk. That tiller steering too: you held it in your left hand and after a while

the continual movement caused a lump at the base of the third finger. 'Following year I got a chance to drive the new Vulcan. That was much better—it had a steering wheel!'

The service was extended southward to Sandbanks with the purchase of the Vulcan, described as 'a 20-seat combined wagonette and charabanc in natural wood': in other words, the seats were fitted lengthwise and laterally. It was registered from the estate office in Poole Road, Westbourne and competed with the omnibus which Eugene Poulain had commenced running 'through' the Canford Cliffs route from the Haven Hotel, Sandbanks to The Square. The first Leyland to be seen in the area joined the Vulcan in May 1908, but the registration of both vehicles was mysteriously cancelled eight months later. Instead, the MMCs soldiered on until January 1909, when they were replaced by two Milnes Daimlers purchased from the Glasgow & South Western Railway Company. These were destined to become the first stage carriage vehicles owned and operated by Bournemouth & District Motor Services Ltd. George Fox was thoroughly impressed:

> They were very good buses, quite the most advanced model available. It was a great treat to drive out of The Square and know she was going to make it up Poole Hill. I used to like the noise of the gears, they hummed along like an electric motor.

With renewed confidence the company stepped up their services and the following timetable—with minor variations—was in use until it was adjusted by Bournemouth & District in 1919:

FROM COUNTY GATES TO CANFORD CLIFFS

9.0., 1.00., 11.0., 11.45., 12.45., 2.15., 3.15., 4.15., 5.0., 6.0., 6.30., 7.15., .930.*

FROM CANFORD CLIFFS TO COUNTY GATES

9.0., 9.45., 10.30., 11.30., 12.15., 2.0., 2.45., 3.45., 5.30., 6.15., 7.0., 9.15.*

* Thursdays only

Fares	Canford Cliffs to County Gates	4d
	„ „ „ Sandbanks	4d
	„ „ „ The Square	6d

Journeys to The Square continued, but in order to protect the trams from competition with large capacity (20 seated) omnibuses, the corporation adopted a policy of granting licences on alternate months—ringing the changes occasionally with lengthier periods. At the other end of the route, further journeys were extended to the Haven Hotel, Sandbanks. The one-and-three-quarter-mile centre section (County Gates to Canford Cliffs) deserves attention, for it is of some historic importance:

> Starting beside a small archway which marked the boundary between the counties of Hampshire and Dorset, the bus moved off into the Avenue and passed beneath the first of the scots pines which line most of the route. After travelling southward for some seven hundred and fifty yards, it turned into Western Road. This carried it past All Saints Church, Branksome and down the western edge of Branksome Chine. Where the road entered the small business centre of Canford Cliffs, the name became Haven Road: here the bus rolled to a halt near the Post Office.

A motor bus first ran along the route in September 1899—and a scheduled service has been advertised ever since. This section, now part of Hants & Dorset's Service No 7, is the oldest motor omnibus service on record to have operated without interruption.

Effective control of the company passed to George Fox in the early days of World War I. He continued to obtain licences to run into Bournemouth on the 'now you have them, now you don't' principle until, on 15 March 1915, the Horse Committee flatly refused to grant any more. Fox withdrew from the section, to concentrate upon that part of the service which now lay under the jurisdiction of Poole Borough Council. He did not change the name of the company and was still running it as such when approached by William Graham. On 20 August 1918, Poole Corporation announced that: 'An application from Bournemouth & District Motor Services Ltd, requesting that licences held by

Mr. G. Fox (Canford Cliffs Motor Company) be transferred to the Company has been granted.'

The following vehicles were operated by the Canford Cliffs Motor Omnibus Company:

Reg No	*Bourne-mouth Licence No*	*Year of Manu-facture*	*Make*	*Type*	*Body*
—	135	1899	MMC	'Canford' 25cwt	8 seat wagonette
—	136	,,	,,	,,	,,
—	154	1900	,,	,,	,,

All were powered by two-cylinder Canstatt-Daimler engines and were tiller steered. On 17 December 1903 they became EL 59–61 respectively and were re-allotted the Bournemouth Licence Nos, 74, 75 and 43.

EL 491	43	1907	Vulcan	30/35hp	Single deck
EL 547	—	1908	Leyland	24/30hp	,,

Bournemouth Licences Nos, 74 and 43 were carried by the two Milnes Daimlers (SD 503–4) between January 1909 and March 1915. These vehicles are described in Chapter Ten.

EUGENE POULAIN

Anxious to secure a solid footing over the entire route between Canford Cliffs and Sandbanks, William Graham was at the same time negotiating the purchase of the service operated by Eugene Poulain of the Haven Hotel, Sandbanks. Although the Poulains spoke good English when it suited them, some little difficulty was encountered: 'How can I discuss the matter with this man?' Graham once appealed, 'He keeps turning to his wife and gabbling away in French and I don't know what they're talking about.' 'My dear Dick', replied the unflappable Mrs Graham, 'I don't suppose he can understand you either!'

Sandbanks was once little more than a fine stretch of golden sand, sparsely covered with clumps of marram grass and a few windswept pines bending away to the north-east. Where the land finally gave way to the tide race at the harbour entrance, there was a small pier from which one could hail a boat for a trip across to Studland. Nearby was the boatman's house and the Haven Hotel. This has its place in history, for it was here that Marconi set up the world's first wireless station in 1901, sending experimental messages to a receiving station on the Isle of Wight. For many years afterward, the original wireless mast remained above the hotel, acting as a minor tourist attraction. The steam-powered omnibus which the engineers had operated in the area doubtless provided the inspiration for the omnibus service between Poole and Sandbanks which was to follow.

The Poole & Sandbanks Motor Omnibus Company Ltd was registered in November 1903, with a capital of £2,000. Although its vehicles were registered in Bournemouth, they were operated from an office at 27 Fish Street, Poole. The first was a 15hp Lifu steam omnibus, resplendent in crimson lake, picked out with black lines and detail work. It commenced running upon the route in March 1904, and was joined by a second slightly heavier machine exactly two months later. The pair proved difficult to operate and maintain and were quickly abandoned: a petrol-engined omnibus being substituted. Registered from the same office in April 1905, this was a bright yellow DeDion two tonner. Seats for the driver and two passengers were provided in the completely open front of the vehicle and the others, for sixteen people, were within a glazed saloon. At the front and back of the roof, reversible boards carried the inscriptions 'to the Haven Hotel' and 'to Poole Park East'.

Latterly, the company name was altered, but then control was gained by the proprietor of the Haven Hotel. Of prime importance to Poulain, was the need to provide efficient transport for people wishing to stay at the hotel. He began to turn his attention toward Bournemouth, whilst maintaining a service from Poole. His initial overtures to Bournemouth Licensing Committee were unsuccessful, but in September 1905, his driver (with the delightful name Alexandre Decressonière) began a schedule of six round trips per day between The Square and the Haven Hotel. Another DeDion was stored throughout the particularly severe winter which followed, for in February 1906, Poulain wrote to *Commercial Motor*:

> We have two buses, both of the DeDion 24hp type. One only is required for the winter service, so the other is at present not in use. The first started running on September 10th 1905 and kept running until January 21st 1906. It was out every day and over very bad roads, for between here and Bournemouth it is all up and down hill and the roads have never been in such a bad state as this winter. The engine has not given out in any way, only two or three sparking plugs required. The bus was only built for 18 persons, but many times we have taken over 25. We do 72 miles per day and use on average seven gallons of petrol. We had no conveyance of any sort before, and find that the use of the bus increases the number of visitors to the hotel. A motor boat is being built, which will run in connection with the omnibuses and I anticipate good results from the attractive combination.

Poulain certainly did obtain those good results, for within a few years he possessed a fleet of motor launches which operated regular services between the Haven Pier and Studland, Shell Bay and Poole. Mme A. Poulain ran the hire section of the business, offering both motor boats and cars, well before World War I. There was competition on the water as well as on land, for J. Harvey of Harbour View House also ran a hire and ferry service which was destined to outlive Poulain's—indeed, it is still going strong at the time of writing. In its pre-war heyday, however, Poulain's 'Sandbanks Motor Car & Ferry Service' was a tremendous success. An eighty-gallon reserve petrol store was provided at the hotel and five more DeDion Boutons were to join the road fleet. These were chars-à-banc with bodies of advanced design specially produced by the Dorsetshire body builders, A. Knight & Company, and used almost exclusively as stage carriage vehicles.

Inevitably, Poulain's route overlapped the service of the Canford Cliffs company. Whilst Fox suffered the usual spasmodic issue of licences on the final leg to Bournemouth, Poulain met greater difficulties. He began to receive refusals on the grounds that he was 'not a resident of Bournemouth'. It is difficult to believe that the number of people he could transport to the hotel on his remote peninsula could have adversely affected the Bournemouth hotel industry, so one must presume that once again, the local tramways were being protected. George Fox, however, who lived just inside the borough boundary at Westbourne, was considered a resident, despite the 'Dorset' name of his business.

Refused licences in the east, Poulain now received overtures from the opposite direction. He was paid a most unusual compliment by Poole Corporation, the Town Clerk officially inquiring whether he would be prepared to re-introduce a service of motor buses along his original route between Park Gates East and Sandbanks. This approach was made three weeks after the commencement of World War I and although Poulain was delighted to oblige, the demands of the military soon forced him to withdraw.

Despite the government's far-sighted subsidy plan for the provision of extra military vehicles, there were still not enough to satisfy the requirements of the army in the area. Accordingly, under the provisions of the Defence of the Realm Act, three of Poulain's DeDions were commandeered in November 1914 for use by the Army Service Corps as lorries in Southampton Docks, where they remained for the duration of the war.

Before the fleet was thus depleted, 'The Sandbanks Motor Car & Ferry Service' timetable for the period 'Easter to 30th September' 1914 was as follows:

FROM COUNTY GATES TO THE HAVEN HOTEL

10.15., 11.15.,* 12.30., 2.30., 3.30., 4.30.,* 6.0., 7.0.
Sunday Service .. 11.0., 2.30., 3·30., 6.0., 7.0.

FROM THE HAVEN HOTEL TO COUNTY GATES

9.45., 10.45.,* 12.0., 3.0., 4.0.,* 5.30., 6.30.
Sunday Service .. 10.30., 2.0., 3.0., 5.30., 6.30.

* From Friday 'til Easter Monday & every day after Whitsuntide

The fares were the same as those charged by the Canford Cliffs Motor Omnibus Company.

The following vehicles were operated by the Poole & Sandbanks Motor Omnibus Company Ltd:

Reg No	*Year of Manu-facture*	*Make*	*Type*	*Body*
EL 159	1904	Lifu	15hp 28cwt steam omnibus	Single deck
EL 162	,,	,,	15hp 35cwt steam omnibus	,,

. . . and by the Sandbanks Motor Car Company Ltd and Eugene Poulain:

EL 273	1905	DeDion Bouton	24hp 40cwt	18 seat Single deck
?	?	,,	,,	,,
FX 776	1910	,,	30hp	28 seat Charabanc
FX 1080	1911	,,	35hp	,,
FX 1546	1913	,,	,,	,,
FX 1870	,,	,,	,,	,,
FX 2139	1914	,,	,,	,,

FX 776 and FX 1546 were acquired by Bournemouth & District and put to work with the ex-Canford Cliffs buses on the County Gates–Sandbanks route in what has been described as 'their original milk-chocolate livery'. They are described in Chapter Ten.

THE FIRST STAGE CARRIAGE SERVICE

The newly acquired vehicles were taken—with no little triumph, but some fears about their reliability—to the garage in St Michael's Road. Push starts were commonplace and once on service, the buses were closely followed by the general manager in a small Singer saloon, well stocked with spare plugs, chains and copper wire. Breakdowns occurred on almost every other journey and one of the first stage carriage drivers for the company, Clarence Adolphus Blake, recalled the triumphant face of his employer appearing alongside with the gleeful shout: 'Well, this is very good. She's been going now for three trips without stopping!' The serious manpower shortage also caused many headaches and at one stage even Mrs Graham's offer of help was not refused: if an employee fell ill, the managing director's wife became a temporary conductress.

Clearly, these elderly buses had to be replaced or supplemented as soon as possible. Yet new vehicles were almost unobtainable. One required a priority certificate or release from the British Mechanical Transport Section, Army Service Corps—and more often than not, was advised instead to try the second-hand dealers. A London BAT Daimler omnibus—dubbed the 'Blacking Box' because it was covered in boot polish advertisements—provided a hard core for the service until W. F. French was able to rustle up further help. The driver was said to have been gassed at Ypres and chosen so that he might benefit from the sea air.

French next arranged the extended loan of two Aldershot & District Daimler buses, which proceeded to give the timetable an unprecedented credibility. Aldershot & District's major contribution had already been made, however: in June 1916, French had engineered the transfer of Albert E. Webster, who had served with the Aldershot company since its birth in 1907. Appointed secretary, Webster was to prove a thoroughly professional 'busman', masterminding much of the expansion programme which was about to begin. It was a post which he was to hold until he became general manager, twenty-nine years later.

THE FOOTHOLD IS GAINED

Following the armistice and confident of success in the near future, considerably larger premises were acquired. William Graham secured the leasehold of 'The Royal Mews', Norwich Avenue and the company moved in on 1 January 1919. The property had been occupied by Charles L. Jensen, a charabanc operator, and an application was made for the transfer of the licences upon which his vehicles had run. But this was refused on the grounds that he had allowed his licences to lapse and the Horse Committee were, in any case, not prepared to exceed the agreed total of charabanc licences, which had been pegged at fifty. Since Bournemouth & District do not appear to have repeated their request, it is unlikely that Jensen's three Halley charabancs were used—although the livery of his vehicles is recorded as having been changed from yellow to aluminium, which would have facilitated their inclusion in the Silver Fleet. For the record, they were EL 1789–90 of 1913 and EL 3090 of 1916—all 35hp three-tonners.

The Royal Mews became the new registered office and headquarters of the company. As the name suggests, they were originally built for horse traffic and the marshalling area remained for many years, the traditional courtyard of setts sloping gently towards a central gutter and drain. To the left of the entrance, two houses formed an integral part of the structure and into these moved the families of William Graham and Albert Webster. At the rear, an orchard lent a rustic air to the property.

Bournemouth & District now set about modernising the premises. A girder-framed glass roof, which considerably amplified the clanking buckets and the cheery whistling of the bus cleaners late into the night, was constructed over the yard. Hand-operated petrol pumps were installed at the head of a sunken tank, racks for vehicle report cards and destination boards appeared around the walls, and an inspection pit was built beneath the level of the setts. Once again, the company set out to obtain permission to operate services befitting its chosen title.

Negotiations with Bournemouth Corporation were re-opened in January 1919. French and Graham personally attended a meeting of the Horse Committee and again put the case for a series of services radiating from Bournemouth. French suggested that, in order to protect the tram service, they would be prepared to charge fares 50 per cent higher than the corporation, whilst operating within the Borough. He pointed out that this had been effective in preventing competition in other towns and relations with the various tramway authorities had been most cordial. There was a direct service from Chatham to Hastings of forty-two miles and before the petrol restrictions had taken effect, the Brighton service ran east to Eastbourne, north to Handcross and west to Portsmouth & Southsea. These were to be resumed with an extension to Southampton and it was planned to link London with the South Coast from Margate to Weymouth—and indeed, the greater part was already covered. A single deck bus of the type proposed was easier to manage than a charabanc. It would not be absolutely necessary to have fixed places for stopping, as this would take less than one minute. The only place requiring a longer stop would be the terminus, which he suggested would be arranged at The Square. William Graham answered the several questions put by committee members and concluded by emphasising that the company did not intend to both pick up and set down the same passenger within the Tramways Department's operating area. This done, the deputation withdrew.

The committee now called upon the Borough Engineer for a report. They were told that the highways within the Borough were neither constructed nor suitable for traffic such as the institution of a motor omnibus service would involve. Furthermore, it was impossible to spend large sums on repairs or alterations to the highways which the normal use of the roads did not require.

A joint meeting of the Horse, Roads and Tramways Committees was arranged and the councillors considered the following points:

(a) The question of the necessity of the proposed service, having regard to:—
  (1) The existing facilities provided by the tramway services to Poole and Christchurch.
  (2) The existing railway facilities to these and the more outlying districts which the proposed omnibuses would serve.
  (3) The service already provided, or to be provided, by the 50 charabancs which the Council had already determined to licence for service between Bournemouth and places within a fairly comprehensive area.

(b) The effect upon the roads of the Borough, to whose upkeep the company proposing to run the services would not directly

contribute. ("As to this, the members will have seen from the recent reports of the Roads Committee, that a very large expenditure is now needed upon the roads owing to their necessary neglect during the period of the war.")
(c) The effect upon the Tramway's permanent way.

The council were particularly sensitive on this last point, for, as a Tramways Committee member put it:

> 'In the near future a large amount of money will have to be spent upon the replacement of the track, owing to the impossibility during the war of maintaining it in an efficient condition. The expense will come at a time when every economic consideration would point to delay—if delay were longer possible.'

Summing up, the Town Clerk reminded the members of the council's powers with regard to omnibuses. The council might licence such a number of omnibuses as they thought fit. The effect of the judgements given in cases in which Blackpool and Brighton Corporations were concerned may well have proven satisfactory, but each case must be considered on its merits. No general rule must be laid down.

The Horse Committee recommended that the application be not entertained for the following reasons:

(a) The opinion of the Borough Engineer, with which the Committee agrees, that the roads of the Borough are not constructed and are not suitable for such additional traffic as the introduction of the proposed scheme would involve.
(b) That the additional service would very seriously and prejudicially affect the amenities of the town from a general traffic point of view.
(c) That it is quite unnecessary, having regard to the facilities already provided by:—
 (1) The London and South Western Railway service.
 (2) The Corporation Tramway service, which will now, under more favourable conditions, very shortly be greatly improved; and
 (3) The service of charabancs which the Council have just recently decided to extend to the licensing of 50 cars.

When the Joint Committee decided to adopt the recommendation, it was clear that this was merely a holding-action in order that the corporation might fully consider their own transport's future under peace-time conditions. They were, after all, not inexperienced in the operation of motor buses and the need to replace and repair large sections of the tramlines had won support for those advocating the substitution of omnibuses. Two motor buses remained in operation and these became the subject of close scrutiny.

With the benefit of hindsight, the reasons offered for refusal do not bear close inspection. The stubborn insistence that the company should really be seeking licences of Class 'A', together with the continual reference to 'the total number of charabancs' just does not ring true. Indeed one of the Joint Committee members was none other than Councillor Bell—and he, more than any other, had full knowledge of the differences between Classes A and B. 'B' licences had been issued in the borough since 1890 for horse-drawn and 1899 for motor vehicles. The Canford Cliffs Motor Omnibus Company's vehicles had been licensed under Class 'B'—and had operated to a point outside the borough. There had been no mention of Class 'A' then. In December 1918, the council, on behalf of the local Chamber of Trade, had pressed the Petrol Control Department to abolish the mileage limit for the town's taxis and substantially increase the allowance of fuel granted for passenger vehicles.

To some extent both sides were hampered by each other's ambiguity. Bournemouth & District were at one and the same time offering to charge fares 50 per cent in excess of the trams, whilst denying their intention to both pick up and set down the same passenger within the Tramways area. For their part, the Horse Committee's Regulations described a charabanc licensed under Class 'A' as:

> 'An omnibus starting within the Borough and going to a place or places outside the Borough and not intended to take up passengers, to be set down on the route taken by such omnibus within the Borough.'

It was this paragraph which substantiated the adamant stand

of the committee. Taken in that literal sense, a charabanc—or a modern touring motor coach, for that matter—could be said to have operated in this fashion, but it was far from an accurate definition of the true purpose of the vehicle.

Almost certainly, the council knew that their stand was being made upon very thin ice, for at the same time they admitted that the bylaws concerned with the licensing of omnibuses were under review. The Horse Committee had in fact retired to consider these with a view to their being brought up to date—and to find a name for itself which better suited the times. Even the pro-motor-omnibus group within the council realised that the Tramways Department could not hope to acquire powers to run omnibuses in the way suggested by Bournemouth & District Motor Services Ltd, and the final discouraging note arrived in the form of the Tramway Manager's Report for the year ending 31 March 1919. Both the Westbourne and Alum Chine bus and that operating between Boscombe Arcade and Boscombe Pier had earned considerably less than the previous year. Since 1916, the two vehicles had returned an annual deficit of over £800. On this occasion, fewer miles had been run, but the loss was said to be due to war bonuses and the extra cost of materials. It was feared that this would have to be met by the electric tramcar receipts.

The very next day, the *Bournemouth Daily Echo* announced:

> A joint meeting of the Horse, Roads and Tramways Committees, after very full consideration, recommended the Council today to enter into communications with the Bournemouth & District Motor Services Ltd., on the subject of their application.

The date, somewhat unkindly perhaps, was 1 April. Later that month, the Lymington & District Motor Service Company Ltd, newly formed in the town of that name, told the council that they proposed to run omnibuses between Lymington and Boscombe—and were informed by return that the Horse Committee were prepared to consider the issue of the necessary licences, on the condition that the special fares they would be expected to charge would apply to the whole of the tramway area and not to the Borough only. The walls had fallen: Bournemouth & District had blown loud and long, yet—at the last—were forced to share the triumphal entry.

At the beginning of July, Bournemouth & District submitted a list of fares which they proposed to charge on the service to Lymington. Lymington & District submitted theirs. The committee recommended that the council grant licences to both companies, but to Lymington & District on the condition that they raise their fares to the same scale as that approved for Bournemouth & District: in other words, that both would charge fares 50 per cent above the trams in their operating area. The stopping places were to be arranged to the satisfaction of the Horse Committee.

But the company were ill-equipped to indulge in competition with so few vehicles available and—apart from familiarisation runs—gave Lymington & District nine months start. Instead, licences were obtained for a pioneer service from The Square to Ringwood Station, which started on 19 July 1919. Bournemouth & District Motor Services Ltd had come home at last!

CHAPTER FOUR

BOURNEMOUTH AND GENERAL PROGRESS

A REAL START

THE ROYAL MEWS now became a hive of enthusiastic activity. Ticket and inquiry offices were built, Samuel Walton was installed as company engineer and Harry Graham, a trained carpenter and brother of the general manager, superintendent of the bodyshop.

In 1919, BAT placed large orders for the Leyland 36/40hp model (the 'N' type, superseded in January 1920 by the 'G5', which was 5in shorter). George Randall, demobilised from the RASC in May 1919, considered them a great advance. Taught to drive by George Fox, he had driven the Milnes Daimlers at Canford Cliffs until his enlistment, and was now engaged by Bournemouth & District to drive an 'N' type charabanc along the same route. The first batch fitted with Dodson CD 19 saloon bodywork was built that year and company drivers were sent to Willesden to collect them. Anxious to place them in service at the earliest moment, the management fell victim to a classic case of 'more haste, less speed'. George Randall relates:

> When we arrived at the body factory, they were still wet and one of their men was actually painting the wings black. Reg Hewlett, who was senior to me, went off to telephone Bournemouth. 'We've got to take them down,' he said, 'I suppose they think we're trying to get a night in London.' So away we came and the roads weren't tar-macadamed then: they were very dusty. Well, I kept as far back from Hewlett's bus as possible, but when we got

home, the buses were plastered. Dust and gnats—just like a fly paper! Harry Graham had to put up tarpaulins and it took his crew a week to rub down and repaint both buses.

The new Leylands were allotted to those companies of the group who had acquired licences for their immediate employ: that Bournemouth & District possessed only five by the end of the year gives some idea of the early frustration felt at the Royal Mews as the management strove to gain some territory. Nevertheless, the company were to acquire thirty-four of the type during the next few years and to it goes the credit for pioneering work on all new routes until the summer of 1924—and several others after that.

Throughout the month following the inauguration of the Ferndown and Ringwood service, only the two Daimlers on hire from Aldershot & District were available to run it, but fortunately it was so popular that the people of St Ives (Hants) eagerly boarded the buses on the outward run and paid the 3d fare into Ringwood—just to be sure of getting a seat on the Bournemouth-bound vehicle.

Four heterogeneous charabancs—in Silver Fleet livery—were fully occupied on the original route from County Gates to Sandbanks and another between Poole and Sandbanks, reinstated at the invitation of Poole Borough Council on 23 May 1919. Conductresses were employed on these two seaside services, but when they left to take up other jobs, an all-male road-crew policy was introduced, mainly for the benefit of ex-servicemen.

In 1920, Thomas Wolsey* representing the Thomas Tilling organisation, joined the board of directors, Tillings were at the time obtaining an interest in each of the BAT subsidiaries—an arrangement which considerably strengthened the hand of the managements concerned. The planned series of advances into the surrounding countryside now began. In January the Poole, Wimborne and Blandford run commenced, to be extended to Shaftesbury two years later. An alternative route to Ringwood and on to Fordingbridge via Christchurch was started, with

* Younger brother to the better known Walter Wolsey.

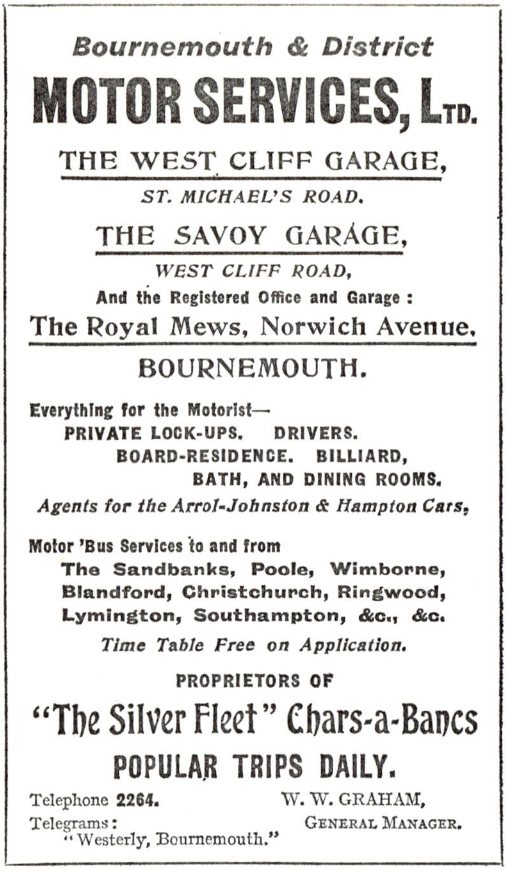

A 1920 advertisement listing the several activities of Bournemouth & District

connections to Salisbury provided by Wilts & Dorset Motor Services Ltd, and on 18 May, permission was granted for the two companies to operate a through service along the combined route between Bournemouth and Salisbury.

The first of the company's timetable cases was erected at the bottom of Avenue Road, Bournemouth: its format becoming standard along all routes until the late thirties. It was the same size and shape as the panels currently used by Western National/ Royal Blue, but was wooden-framed and glass-fronted. Setting up these cases was not the simple matter one might imagine: some country folk viewed the new services with disfavour. The company then relied upon local employees to allay such apprehensive opposition. George Randall, now promoted:

> I remember I went and asked at a grocer's shop in Ferndown, if we could put a timetable case on his wall. He said to me, 'No, you'll take business from me—into Ringwood and Bournemouth.' 'Oh no,' I said, 'we shall bring it. You must link places up: it works both ways. All the people at Ferndown—their relations will be coming out on Sunday to see Mum and Dad and they'll come down to you and buy more food. You'll find that your business will grow.' Later on, that man said to me, 'You were quite right, indeed right, my trade is better than it was', and up went our case. 'Well, goodbye Mr. Graham', he said. 'Oh, I'm not the general manager,' I said, 'I'm an inspector.'

In March came the news which at one and the same time ensured the eventual monopoly of the Lymington route and set in motion the major expansion into eastern Hampshire: a small operator in Southampton had agreed to sell his charabancs and—more important—his premises. This transaction and the events which followed are described in Chapter Five, but one result of this move must be mentioned here. Rather than face an outcry of the kind suffered by the London & Southampton Railway (when Portsmouth learned that it was about to be served by a branch of the railway so-named, their protests resulted in the substitution of the title 'London & South Western Railway'), the company decided to change their own name, lest the citizens of Southampton, in their turn, were likewise offended. On 27 July 1920, the company assumed its present title—Hants & Dorset Motor Services Ltd.

Later that year, permission was forthcoming from the Dorchester and Poole authorities for a through service to Weymouth, but once again, the spectre of home-based competition with the trams resulted in a refusal from Bournemouth, whilst a rival concern, the Weymouth Motor Company Ltd, were given the go-ahead. For a brief period, Hants & Dorset ran along the stretch between Poole and Dorchester, but withdrew as their long-range competitor 'captured the road'—and many years were to elapse before they returned.

Meanwhile, increasing numbers of Leyland saloons were delivered and the crews began to build up a reputation for courtesy and care, which has been their hall-mark ever since. Those who scrambled for the honour of sitting beside the driver in the forward compartment soon established the custom of rewarding him with gifts of fruit, chocolate or produce, whilst the regulars proved most useful by showing a new driver the roads to be taken. A great deal of self-sufficiency was expected of the crews: in the event of a breakdown, the driver did his best to get the bus moving. He was equipped with the key to a veritable treasure chest, for this was the repair kit issued with all new Leyland 'N' and 'G5' types:

1 spanner 1″ and $1\frac{1}{8}$″	1 tail lamp bracket
,, $\frac{7}{8}$″ ,, $\frac{3}{4}$″	2 side ,, ,,
,, $\frac{13}{16}$″ ,, $\frac{11}{16}$″	1 sparking plug
,, $\frac{5}{8}$″ ,, $\frac{1}{2}$″	2 valve springs
,, $\frac{7}{16}$″ ,, $\frac{3}{8}$″	1 back brake spring
,, $\frac{5}{16}$″ ,, $\frac{1}{4}$″	1 screwdriver
,, $\frac{11}{16}$″ ,, $\frac{9}{16}$″	1 axle spanner
1 box spanner $\frac{7}{16}$″/$\frac{1}{2}$″	1 bottle jack
1 oil can	1 'C' clutch spanner
1 hand hammer	1 funnel
1 valve tube	1 key for magneto
1 length of copper wire	1 spare valve and washer
1 pair of pliers	1 wrench for wheel cap oil plug
1 chisel	1 spanner for valve covers
1 6″ half-round file	1 dozen assorted split pins
1 horn and bulb	1 renewal bracket

If this formidable array proved insufficient, there was little else the unfortunate crew could do than await the arrival of another bus from the depot. In the event of a ditching, there were no breakdown vehicles available to help and one of the buses or the nearest farm tractor was called upon to perform the extraction.

At the Royal Mews, just as much effort was required of the office staff—particularly when heavy Bank Holiday and high-summer traffic caught the company short-handed. On several occasions, all were required to work in other departments and secretary A. E. Webster was often to be found helping in the ticket office. If, however, the returns for a Bank Holiday period were particularly good—and they usually were—all crews were rewarded with a bonus of up to ten shillings.

Initially, a peaked cap and badge were all that the company could afford to issue, but these were soon followed by overcoats or raincoats and leggings for the drivers. The latter were particularly useful in the original Dodson-bodied Leylands, for the cabs were open to the weather above the waistrail. Weatherproof clothing was also provided for relief crews required to go by company motorcycle to take-over buses working on isolated routes, and for 'outside inspectors' who also used motorcycles.

AN ARRANGEMENT WITH ROYAL BLUE

In the spring of 1921, John T. G. Elliott of Elliott Brothers 'Royal Blue', together with his general manager H. W. Rollings and Bournemouth motor dealer W. J. Snelgrove, visited a British military depot at Le Havre and browsed among the Daimler and AEC 'Y' type lorries languishing there. The Royal Blue shoppers picked out fourteen units and had them shipped back to England. The Daimler works made up a dozen sound units from the batch and forwarded them to Christopher Dodson Ltd, builders of the current Hants & Dorset saloon bodies. Elliott Brothers next applied for (and were granted, on 21 July 1921) licences to operate four vehicles each, on stage carriage services to Lymington, Wimborne and Ringwood, in direct competition with those already worked by Hants & Dorset. Whilst a stunned management met at the Royal Mews to discuss ways of meeting this unexpected challenge, the managing director of Royal Blue became seriously ill and spent an extensive period in Switzerland to recuperate. This seems to have taken the steam out of the entire plan, for it was not until October 1923, that his brother Henry H. Elliott renewed the application. On this occasion, the committee declared that since other applications had been received and dealt with in respect of these routes and that the original was made so long ago, they were not prepared to grant this large number of additional licences, and considered the original application to have lapsed. One wonders, therefore, why the transaction which followed was necessary, but transaction there was.

By now the vehicles were fast becoming superb elderly specimens, little used. Yet Dodson had endowed each with their latest 'patent applied for' Charabus bodies, the centre sections of the roofs being canvas which could be rolled up to a central beam, and the windows removed and stored beneath the chassis. The result was a genuine 'go there in the sunlight as a charabanc and come back at night as a fully lit and enclosed saloon' bus. On 18 December 1923, it was announced that Hants & Dorset were to take delivery of all twelve from the Dodson works at Willesden. Nine Charabuses duly arrived in Bournemouth, where three were put to work on the Sandbanks route, and the others were delivered at Southampton. All were then registered for the first time.

The agreement which accompanied their acquisition was sealed on 1 February 1924: Hants & Dorset made over to Elliott Brothers £7,500 in cash and £4,400 in fully paid £1 shares and promised that for a period of 21 years, neither the company nor its directors would operate or take an interest in any coaches for tours or express work, taxi cabs or private hire cars. Furthermore, the company were to become booking agents for Royal Blue tours in the area, secure for Elliott Brothers any order for the hire of private cars, grant first opportunity for the provision by Royal Blue of relief vehicles for stage carriage work, and provide free advertising space in the Small Car Depot at the West Cliff Garage. The company could continue to store visitors' cars, but were no longer free to hire out their own.

For their part, Elliott Brothers promised not to take an interest in stage carriage services in the agreed Hants & Dorset area. When the deal was settled, both parties felt that the decks had been cleared for their own range of action. Hants & Dorset had obviously taken the challenge very seriously and, as later developments proved, done well to leave themselves in a good bargaining position when Poole decided to take up the tramlines. On the other side of the coin, Royal Blue were now free to set up long-distance coach services without having to look over their shoulders for home-based competition.

NEW ROUTES AND ACQUISITIONS

For two years, the contest between the company and the Lymington & District Motor Service hung in the balance. In the early days, much of the revenue was taken by Lymington & District who, because they operated no other services, were able to place the full weight of their effort upon the route. Their fleet of AEC 'YC' type saloons offered the same carrying capacity as the Hants & Dorset buses and were first-class equipment. Because of their commitments on other routes, the company were at first hard-put to counter their undoubted popularity. In order that they might gain an extra journey in the mornings, Hants & Dorset stationed one Leyland overnight at a garage in New Street, Lymington and, as the Bournemouth fleet began to build up to something like eighteen vehicles, this move led to the establishment of a depot at Lymington.

In 1924, the motorbus and charabanc business of S. W. & C. L. Bushby of Wallisdown was purchased. Their small capacity buses were immediately replaced by 34-seaters and the service—between Talbot Road, Winton and Wallisdown—was stepped up to twenty-six journeys per day. Four journeys were extended to the village of East Howe and two to Bourne Hill, to make connections with the Shaftesbury bus coming north from Poole. Between September and December 1926, an additional route was worked which started at the Wallisdown Liberal Club, went the length of Columbia Road and terminated in Ensbury Park Road. Twenty return journeys per day were operated on this section, the combined service starting and ending inside the Borough of Bournemouth. By the spring of 1927, the Bourne Hill and Ensbury Park Road extensions had been withdrawn, whilst the surviving

Winton, Wallisdown and East Howe route became No 9 in the series issued that year.

January 1925 saw the arrival of the first forward-control half-cab vehicles, a configuration which offered greater carrying capacity, but banished the 'front riders' from their usual travelling place. These were the large Leyland 'SG9' type, still fitted with solid tyres and spoked wheels. A bulkhead divided the saloon into two compartments: the smokers being requested to sit at the rear. Several drivers have recalled early morning runs with most of the passengers crowding into the rear compartment for the traditional breakfast cigarette and making the vehicle so unstable that if a humped back bridge were crossed, practically all steerage-way was momentarily lost. Nevertheless, they were the ideal tool along the heavily populated routes and did well on the roads to Ringwood and Lymington. Along both there was competition with local men operating two vehicles apiece.

The licences of J. G. Robertson and A. G. Kingswell were transferred to the company after a rather one-sided battle and Mr Kingswell became an employee. This 'victory' was an achievement of the first small-capacity Morris 'One Ton' 13-seater, whose purpose was to tail a competitor's bus and either overtake it in a burst of speed at the spots most likely to offer the larger pockets of custom, or merely roll to a halt behind the other and woo the passengers with reduced fares. Depending on one's point of view, this was unfortunately the only occasion upon which the type was successful. Elsewhere, the 'chaser' as it was aptly dubbed, did little else than chase. If a competitor was using good equipment, it was neither fast enough to overtake, nor even to keep pace. Drivers of such a 'chaser' found this mildly humiliating and were greatly relieved when the Morris' were sent to do more leisurely work in sparsely populated areas.

Hants & Dorset Motor Services Ltd became a public company in July 1924, by which time both staff and crews had captured the affection and support of the travelling majority. Twinn Brothers of Pokesdown were commissioned to design and make a series of rustic shelters to be located at the more exposed bus stops. The wooden rooms were tailor-made to suit the sites and were extensively decorated with half-round timbers. In some cases, the company went so far as to provide park benches and plant tubs to round off the cosy effect.

William Graham's personal prestige now began to soar with that of his company. He became chairman of the Motor & Engineering Section of the Bournemouth Chamber of Trade. During his year of office, H. H. Elliott was the vice-chairman and the two began to forge an understanding which led to further co-operation at a later date. In 1923, Graham became vice-chairman of the Chamber of Trade and, at a meeting in the municipal college the following February, was unanimously elected president. During his presidential year, he entertained Sir Thomas Lipton during the Bournemouth Yachting Regatta and supervised the production of a publicity film for Bournemouth.

Periodically, throughout the first half of the twenties, the small figure of Walter Flexman French was to be seen at the company's offices. In his capacity as chairman, he visited the newly opened depots at Southampton, Lymington and Gosport, offering words of advice and encouragement to the staff. On one such visit to the bodyshop at the Royal Mews, he fingered two stout pieces of timber and remarked upon the quality of the woodwork in modern bus-building. 'I didn't have the nerve to tell him that they were a pair of clothes posts for Mr Graham', said master coach-builder Arthur Watts. 'After all, he was the chairman!'

French was always full of enthusiasm for the company. 'When we have thirty bus routes, I shall consider Hants & Dorset an operational entity', he once said to William Graham. It was a wish he never saw fulfilled, for he suffered a fall in November 1925 and died the following year at the age of 69 years. To William Graham's everlasting regret, Hants & Dorset were at the time operating twenty-nine routes.

THE GENERAL STRIKE

At the start of the general strike in 1926, Bournemouth Corporation invited volunteers to enlist at the Town Hall, to drive some of the trams—a seemingly dangerous stop-gap. The employees of Hants & Dorset were not obliged to withdraw their labour, for none were then members of a trade union. The company therefore provided a series of emergency services along the tramway routes at the request of the corporation—such is the irony of fate! Several of Elliott Brothers' pneumatic-tyred charabancs performed similar duties, but most Hants & Dorset buses were still on solids: it was not until 1927 that these began to enter the shops to be re-shod.

LOWER PARKSTONE ET ALIBI

In 1928, Hants & Dorset were granted permission to commence running a new series of services within the Borough of Poole. These offered a 3d ride from Alder Road, Branksome to Wallisdown, twenty-three journeys per day between Newtown, Poole and Upton and, most important, a service between the George Hotel, Poole and County Gates—six per day via Lilliput and the other two via Lower Parkstone. The latter brought Hants & Dorset buses into direct competition with Bournemouth Corporation tramcars for the first time, although these were, of course, running on tracks under the control of Poole Borough. These tracks were due for replacement—always a costly business—and the efficiency of the bus services so recently introduced, did not go unnoticed.

That same year, Poole obtained authority to close the Lower Parkstone line and introduce in its stead, a service of motor buses which could be run along any route up to a distance of 10 miles from Poole Railway Station. Rather than purchase vehicles of their own, Poole Corporation entered into an agreement with Hants & Dorset for the provision of a replacement service. (See Chapter Six.) Furthermore, Poole promised not to operate its own services for a period of 7 years from the passing of the local Act (3 July 1928), by which time the whole question of road transport within the borough would be reviewed.

The Lower Parkstone service commenced running in January

Page 69 (*above*) Twinn Brothers of Pokesdown were commissioned to design and make rustic shelters to be sited at rural bus stops; (*below*) A Leyland SG9—the smoking compartment at the rear proved so popular, that the front wheels tended to lift from the ground

Page 70 (above) Hants & Dorset's first new double deckers—delivered in 1926—were Leyland GH7 open-toppers with Brush bodywork

(left) An acquired AEC with 'Charabus' type bodywork at The Red Lion, Bursledon in 1925

(below) This Leyland PLSC3 'Lion', with its roof luggage rack and ladder is a typical late 'Twenties' saloon

1929 with a fleet of Leyland TD 1 'Titan' open-toppers with Short Brothers bodywork, the first journey being a tree lopping session along the route. Within weeks, the company also had available 'Titans' with full-height enclosed bodywork, but since Bournemouth Corporation's trams were all open-topped, only two of these were permitted to run on the Lower Parkstone route, and then only as relief vehicles during the rush hour. Fortunately, twelve 'Titans' fitted with Leyland bodywork in the new 'lowbridge' configuration were delivered soon after. Although these still featured outside staircases, the total height of each vehicle had been reduced by constructing a sunken gangway along the off-side of the upper deck and arranging most of the seats in rows of four. Despite the compensatory bulge in the ceiling below—just right for banging one's head, when leaving the seat—this type was duly authorised for full use upon the Lower Parkstone route, and buses of 'lowbridge' design were to become a feature of Hants & Dorset, until the last was phased out in 1972.

It was now possible to travel between The Square and Poole on a company bus for 5d: previously, a protective fare had been charged along the section on the services to Wareham and to Shaftesbury. Indeed, the fare on the former and a through service to Dorchester and Weymouth which started the following year, was pegged at 8d. The Shaftesbury service was now re-routed by way of Winton, Moordown and Kinson, and to retain the link with Poole, nine journeys per day were run from a new depot there, connecting at Bear Cross. This alteration had scarcely been put to effect, when the new section was subjected to some unexpected opposition.

IMPERIAL MOTOR SERVICES

Preoccupied with events 'over the border', the management were now surprised by the arrival of a new competitor who set up shop on their own doorstep. Mr & Mrs Alfred J. Wilkins arrived from Wales in 1928 and took a hotel in Sea Road, Boscombe. Hardly likely to cause the company any concern; but what was not known at the time was that the Wilkins had operated an omnibus service at Aberdare, had sold out to Red & White and arrived in Bournemouth with the express purpose of starting afresh. They obtained a licence to run between The Square and Wimborne via Canford, and by the summer of the following year, were running six AECs and two Star 'Flyer' saloons. The Wimborne route was then extended to Blandford Forum, in competition with Hants & Dorset's service to Shaftesbury. An alternative route to Bournemouth was opened via Ferndown, whilst the Star 'Flyers' were purchased in July to operate a connecting service from Ringwood and West Moors. A garage for four vehicles was opened in Leigh Road, Wimborne and the rest were maintained at Boscombe. This high-powered fleet—even the Stars were six-cylinder models—was a good match for the 'Lions' which were ranged against it and the company's fortunes on the Wimborne road reached their nadir by the autumn.

Two factors eventually swung the battle Hants & Dorset's way: a pair of extremely fast Leyland TS2 'Tigers' joined forces with the 'Lions' in September 1929, whilst the direct route to Ferndown via New Road at Ensbury, which had been metalled the previous year, remained the company's preserve. As the competition intensified, so the fares spiralled downward: what was originally a 1s 6d (7½p) return fare between Bournemouth and Wimborne was being offered at 6d (2½p) in the spring of 1930. This, the company's last great 'battle' for custom—fought like the first against a fleet of AECs—was probably the fiercest: let it suffice to say that one 'Lion' came to rest in Leigh Pond at Wimborne after a particularly vigorous exchange. Imperial Motor Services sold out to Hants & Dorset on 20 May 1930—the AECs being used but briefly until further buses were delivered.

THE SOUTHERN RAILWAY INTEREST

On 1 January 1923, the old LSWR was absorbed within one of the four newly-formed main-line companies, the Southern Railway. The management of the new company became preoccupied with reorganisation in general, and the further development of Southampton Docks and London suburban electrification extensions in particular. Thus, despite the fact that the motor bus had become an increasingly serious competitor, five years were to elapse before positive steps were taken to acquire a share of the profits from this form of transport. The Southern Railway, in concert with the other three, decided to seek parliamentary powers to run omnibuses, a technicality which had been conveniently ignored by the constituent LSWR, who—like Southampton Corporation in 1900 and 1901—had briefly operated stage carriage services in Hampshire which, strictly speaking, were illegal. The appropriate sanction was granted under the provisions of the Southern Railway (Road Transport) Act 1928, but strictures laid down by the Ministry of Transport made this something of a potential pyrrhic victory: if the Southern had chosen to run its own buses, it could not have hoped to compete upon even terms with the existing Tilling & BAT companies. Accordingly, the four main-line companies decided to buy themselves into the existing industry.

Negotiations with Tilling & BAT began in November 1928, but were complicated by the railway companies' successful efforts to invest in other omnibus companies. For example, Hants & Dorset's neighbours in the West, the National Omnibus & Transport Company Ltd, had its numerous operations in England divided into companies with a distinct railway flavour: in the South West, the Southern and Great Western Railways lent part of their titles to the ex-NO & T bus services operated in the vicinity of their lines by the new Southern and Western National Omnibus Companies respectively.

Hard bargaining between Tilling & BAT and the London & North Eastern Railway over the latter's proposed outright purchase of the large United Automobile Services Ltd, eventually led to an agreement to make a joint offer for that company: and in October 1929, this arrangement became the basis for the railway companies—either jointly or individually—acquiring shares equal to those of Tilling & BAT in the appropriate omnibus companies. Thus the Southern Railway invested individually in the

Aldershot & District, East Kent, Hants & Dorset, Maidstone & District, Southdown, Southern Vectis and Wilts & Dorset omnibus companies—and jointly with the GWR in Thames Valley. The Southern paid 45 shillings (£2.25) each for their Hants & Dorset shares and two of their representatives joined the board of directors.

From the travelling public's point of view there was at first very little to show for it. It was not until the summer of 1930 that the company's timetables declared it to be 'In association with the Southern Railway Coy' and displayed the London train times, and not before 1932 that the train services between Bournemouth, Southampton and Winchester were featured. True, some buses were sent off to meet the trains, the most noteworthy instance being the extension of the Ringwood and Burley service to Holmsley Station in August 1930, but the managing director must have forgotten that this was where Grandfather Francis had started the ball rolling, for without a trace of affection, this historic revival was terminated at the end of that year. First mention of Hants & Dorset in railway publicity came in December 1932, when it was named as providing Sunday transport between Brockenhurst and Lymington. Equally difficult to unearth are early road/rail interavailability arrangements. Not until one has perused the small print in 'Passenger Regulations' for June 1935, may one find that:

> The contract entered into by the Company is limited to the carriage of the passenger by road. If a passenger holding a return ticket desires to return by railway in cases where special arrangements for such returns exist, he will, on presenting such a ticket at a railway station, be given the opportunity of entering into a contract with the Railway Company entitling him to return by train on payment of the appropriate supplement (if any) and subject to the Railway Company's conditions.

Such facilities were first offered between Poole–Broadstone or Wimborne and Lyndhurst Road Station–Southampton, but a complete list was not published in the company timetable until another seven years had elapsed and the country was again at war.

BOUNDARY CHANGES

On 1 April 1931, under the provisions of the Bournemouth Corporation Act, 1930, the borough boundary was pushed westwards to encompass the villages and housing estates of Wallisdown, East and West Howe, Cudnell, Kinson and Ensbury—all previously in Dorset. In anticipation of this adjustment, the corporation had sought powers to considerably extend their bus services, both within and outside the Borough, but following a petition by Hants & Dorset against this aspect of the Bill, had amended their requirements. The company had therefore withdrawn its petition and agreed that the Winton–Wallisdown–East Howe service should be transferred to the municipality at the end of November 1930. Corporation buses would now operate as far as Bear Cross via Moordown and from Christchurch Town Hall to Purewell: both new routes to be considered part of the 'Corporation Area'. Hants & Dorset were to assess the average annual net profit culled from their Winton–Wallisdown, the Square–Bear Cross, The Square–Christchurch and Christchurch–Purewell services during the two years ending 31 March 1929; and receive, from the corporation, four times that figure as compensation. Furthermore, save when running over the tram routes—where the company were to continue charging the usual excess—Hants & Dorset were to charge any passenger both taken up and set down within the corporation area, the same fare as would have been charged by the corporation—but retain only the operating costs (see Appendix C): the rest to be paid to the corporation in accumulated amounts every six months.

Corporation inspectors were empowered to board Hants & Dorset buses to check a special range of tickets, overprinted 'BCT', which were supplied to the company by the corporation. These underwent only minor modification over the years and remained in use until 31 December 1970.

THE OMNIBUS STATION

By the late twenties, the stands around The Square had become overburdened by both touring coaches and service buses. Fortunately for all concerned, the understanding forged at both personal and company level between Hants & Dorset and Elliott Brothers now resolved the problem: the outcome being the decision to build a joint omnibus and coach station to the south of The Square, on a site previously used by visiting fairs. At first glance, the sloping ground looked unsuitable, but the architects—Jackson & Greenen—designed an ingenious two-tier structure which actually exploited it. The entrances of the wedge-shaped building were at the narrow end, on the junction of Exeter Road with Exeter Lane (later Pavilion Road), facing The Square. A semi-subterranean circulating area was provided for Royal Blue with entrance and exit upon each side of a large ramp leading to the floor above. At the head of this ramp lay the circulating area for Hants & Dorset's stage carriage service buses, with a waiting room at the centre. From the latter, a wide staircase led to the coach station beneath.

The premises were opened to the public on Sunday, 8 March 1931 and from that date all Bournemouth-bound Hants & Dorset buses terminated there, instead of the roadside stands. The new building did much to enhance the reputation of both companies and proved an immediate success with the travelling public. Whether one was swept up the ramp in a bus, or lowered into the depths in a coach, there was little doubt that one had arrived in Bournemouth!

With further traffic resulting from the new routes gained in Poole during 1928, the County Gates stand had now become seriously overcrowded. It was decided to build a small omnibus station and sub-office among the rhododendron bushes, and this was duly opened in the autumn of 1932. Whilst many of the local services terminated there it served its purpose well, but with the granting of 'through running' rights in 1935, its importance gradually diminished and it was eventually closed in 1953.

THE 1935 AGREEMENT

When word reached the Royal Mews that Bournemouth were to review the future of their tramway system, Tilling & BAT gave Hants & Dorset the go-ahead to bid for the right to replace it with company buses, as had already happened with the Lower Parkstone route. But the Tramways Committee had already decided to try trolleybus operation and sought to establish an experimental system. Despite objections lodged by Hants & Dorset and various motoring interests, the appropriate wiring was carried out and trials began in May 1933. These were, of course, successful and led to the setting up of a complete network of trolleybus routes in Bournemouth and Christchurch.

Poole, however, posed a different problem: the agreement by which Bournemouth Corporation leased the tramlines between County Gates and Poole Railway Station was due for renewal in 1935. Hants & Dorset approached Poole council. The outcome —described later—resulted in the company providing buses for practically all the stage carriage work within that borough.

Since Hants & Dorset were now providing all the services between The Square and Poole, the company entered into a revised agreement with Bournemouth Corporation, that—for a period of 40 years—passengers could be both picked up and set down on the same journey, within the prescribed area, upon terms of accountability in respect of the total number involved and for a fixed sum of £1,000 per annum: the 'Corporation Area' it was agreed, extended 440 yards beyond the borough boundary, except at County Gates. Hants & Dorset were no longer required to charge a 50 per cent excess when running over tram routes (or their replacement trolleybus routes); a condition which had been held in force by the 1930 agreement and—for the first time—joint-running return tickets were added to the BCT series, for use on either operator's buses.

Sheer weight of numbers at Bournemouth bus station now

forced the purchase of additional land at the rear of the premises. This expansion proved most timely, for the acquisition of Elliott Brothers' 'Royal Blue' Excursion Department in 1935 and the resumption of tours, meant that this area could be used as a start-point for the coaches. Up to and including the year 1939, some forty coaches were based there and at the newly acquired Pavilion Garage in Bath Road. The marshalling area was later concreted and, in 1937, the rear wall of the station breached, permitting buses to enter the building as their departure times drew near, pick up the passengers under cover—and leave via the front exit. This mode of operation was to prove satisfactory until well after World War II.

One other operator's licence and vehicles were acquired in January 1937; E. H. Saunder's 'Verwood Motor Service'. His two Reo saloons were rather elderly and therefore sold without further use. It proved to be the last pre-war acquisition in the Bournemouth depot's area.

SUMMARY OF ROUTE COMMENCEMENT DATES

(a)	(b)	(c)		
8	29b	12a	Bournemouth–Ferndown–Ringwood	July 1919
10	—	—	,, –Poole–Wimborne	Dec 1919
10	—	—	,, – ,, – ,, –Blandford	Jan 1920
7	17	38	,, –Christchurch–Ringwood	,, ,,
2	20	20	,, – ,, –Lymington	Mar 1920
7	17	38	,, – ,, –Fordingbridge	,, ,,
7	17	38	,, –Fordingbridge–Salisbury	May 1920
—	30	12	,, –Ferndown–West Moors	Oct 1920
10	29	24	,, –Blandford–Shaftesbury	Dec 1921
11	10	89	,, –Poole–Wareham	May 1923
9	—	—	Winton–Wallisdown (1)	July 1924
5	19	15	Bournemouth–Burley–Ringwood	Jan 1926
—	—	—	Wallisdown–Columbia Rd–Ensbury Pk Rd (2)	Sept 1926
12a	7	7	Bournemouth–Sandbanks–Swanage	Apr 1927
—	2	2	,, –Lower Parkstone–Poole	Jan 1929

—	11	11	,,	-Dorchester-Weymouth	Sept 1930
—	—	—	,,	-Portland-Southwell (3)	Jan 1931
—	1/5	1/5	Poole Tramway replacements routes		Jun 1935

(1) Relinquished in favour of Bournemouth Corpn. Nov 1930
(2) Discontinued December 1926
(3) Relinquished in favour of Southern National Sept 1933

Route number series introduced: (a) 1927; (b) 1940; (c) 1946

CHAPTER FIVE

THE SOUTHAMPTON DEPOT 1920–1939

EARLY SOUTHAMPTON BUSES

As soon as the service to Lymington had been sanctioned, Bournemouth & District sought to extend eastward to Southampton and beyond. Again, the company were not the first to run motor omnibuses in the area; an honour which had fallen to Southampton Corporation Tramways Department. Much influenced by the motor wagonettes at Bournemouth, they had experimented unsuccessfully with a hired MMC 'Granville' in August 1900 and a 12-seat Daimler which they bought the following year, thus becoming the first municipality to try the new form of transport. Nineteen years later, the department had recovered sufficient nerve to try again and a fleet of Thornycroft open-toppers was already at work when Bournemouth & District's Leylands eventually arrived in the town.

One of the earliest references to omnibuses in Southampton is to be found in William White's *History, Gazetteer and Directory of Hampshire & the Isle of Wight*, published in June 1859. He mentions services by unnamed horse-bus operators to Bitterne, West End, Hamble, Romsey, Portswood and Swaythling, the Conveyance Company's and Gallop's omnibuses to Shirley and William Duke's to Meonstoke.

Tramways were laid in the streets of the town in 1878 by the 'Southampton Tramways Company' and the cars ran unopposed until 1887, when a Mr Andrews of Cardiff started a rival horse bus service. The Tramways Company bought him out and retained the buses for feeder services. Southampton Corporation acquired the undertaking after lengthy discussions which began in 1895, electrifying the tramway at the turn of the century.

Seven years after the failure of the original motor buses, the corporation again toyed with similar plans. In February 1908, the Sussex Motor Road Car Company Ltd, who had just reached Portsmouth from their base at Worthing, got wind of this and forwarded proposals for running a limited number of their Milnes-Daimler open-toppers along the Northam and Clock Tower route. Their offer was declined and the company soon afterward went into liquidation. In conjectural mood, one may recall that the Sussex Company was soon resurrected by A. Douglas Mackenzie as Worthing Motor Services Ltd, and was absorbed by the newly-formed Southdown Motor Services Ltd in 1915. If the corporation had entertained the 1908 proposals, Southampton would almost certainly have become Southdown territory. Given a strong foothold in the town, BAT would have seen little purpose in planning the establishment of another large company just the other side of the New Forest. Eventually, Southdown would have served the South Coast from Hastings to Weymouth.

Southampton's first motor charabanc was placed in service by W. Johnson & Son Ltd, in March 1914, but the war cut short the venture. It had been backed in committee by an early Southampton motorist, Councillor S. Tebbutt, who was later to enter that field himself and play a most important part in the first footing of Bournemouth & District in the town of Southampton.

The negotiations which were to ensure the future operation of Hants & Dorset buses in the area began before the corporation Thornycrofts appeared on the streets. Walter Flexman French was sure that it was but a matter of time before the restrictions imposed by the Local Government (Emergency Provisions) Order were lifted and, whilst leaving William Graham to pursue their case with Bournemouth, sought to gain a foothold farther east.

On 16 June 1919, the Southampton Watch Committee considered an application from 'French's Garage & Motor Works Ltd.', for licences to run services from 'Southampton to Southsea,

Winchester, Romsey, Salisbury, Bournemouth and the intermediate villages'. French attended this meeting and proposed that he should be granted thirty-six licences. It was resolved that, subject to the recognised 6d minimum fare regulation being observed, the council should be recommended to grant the application.

The ball was now in French's court: the council had intimated that they were prepared to grant the licences, but the truth of the matter was—the company just did not possess that number of buses, nor did it seem likely that they would for many months. A base from which to operate the proposed services had not yet been secured either: the Roller Skating Rink in Shirley Road was very nearly acquired, but this deal was never finalised. The months dragged on; by January 1920 the company owned six Leyland 'N' saloons and it was arranged that three of these should be inspected by the Hackney Carriage Sub-Committee with a view to their being operated to Winchester, Romsey and Bournemouth. The vehicles were found to be in perfect mechanical order: indeed, they represented the finest equipment available, but further matters now conspired to delay their entry into service. The Ministry of Transport Act, 1919 had amended several clauses of the Emergency Provisions Act and was—in part—intended to smooth the way for the general expansion of bus services, but it also provided for the imposition of reasonable conditions by the local authorities in order to protect the ratepayers. Unfortunately, in many areas, fledgling bus companies were faced forthwith by excessive demands for a contribution, based upon mileage, towards the upkeep of the roads. In some cases this was met by a well-publicised withdrawal of the application, to be resubmitted at a later date with the backing of public demand. By comparison, Southampton's request was mild: licences would be granted if payment of 2d per mile were made towards the maintenance of the roads. Nevertheless, the company were not prepared to accede and, despite the cordial tone of the meetings which followed, each inconclusive session served to put back the commencement date a further month.

In March 1920, a company official was permitted to fix a timetable case to the railings at the Above-Bar Street end of Sussex

HANTS AND DORSET MOTOR SERVICES.

NOTICE.

SERVICE of MOTOR OMNIBUSES

BETWEEN

SOUTHAMPTON & LYMINGTON.

On and after SATURDAY, FEB. ~~14~~ 18th, 1920,

DAILY (Sundays Included) and until further notice Motor Omnibuses will run as follows:

		a.m.	p.m.	p.m.
Lymington (Londesborough Hotel)	**dep.**	**9.0**	**12.30**	**4.15**
New Inn	,,	**9.13**	**2.43**	**4.28**
Brockenhurst	,,	**9.25**	**12.55**	**4.40**
Lyndhurst	,,	**9.45**	**1.15**	**5.0**
Lyndhurst Road Station		**10.0**	**1.30**	**5.15**
Hounsdown	,,	**10.6**	**1.36**	**5.21**
Totton	,,	**10.13**	**1.43**	**5.28**
Southampton (Sussex Road, Above Bar)	**arr.**	**10.30**	**2.0**	**5.45**

		a.m.	p.m.	p.m.
Southampton (Sussex Road Above Bar)	**dep.**	**10.35**	**2.10**	**6.15**
Totton	,,	**10.52**	**2.27**	**6.32**
Hounsdown	,,	**10.59**	**2.34**	**6.39**
Lyndhurst Road Station		**11.5**	**2.40**	**6.45**
Lyndhurst	,,	**11.20**	**2.55**	**7.0**
Brockenhurst	,,	**11.40**	**3.15**	**7.20**
New Inn	,,	**11.52**	**3.27**	**7.32**
Lymington (Londesborough Hotel)	**arr.**	**12.5**	**3.40**	**7.45**

Fares.

	Lymington	New Inn	Brockenhurst	Lyndhurst	Lyndhurst Road Station	Hounsdown	Totton
New Inn	4d.						
Brockenhurst	8d.	4d.					
Lyndhurst	1 4	1 -	8d.				
Lyndhurst Road Station	1 10	1 6	1 2	6d.			
Hounsdown	2 -	1 8	1 4	8d.	2d.		
Totton	2 3	1 10	1 6	10d.	4d.	2d.	
Southampton	2 9	2 6	2 2	1 6	1/-	10d.	8d.

Pending the erection of a Garage at Southampton the above Service will be operated by the Bournemouth & District Motor Services, Ltd.

They will make every effort to maintain the Service but give no guarantee that the same will be performed, and reserve the right to alter or revise the Time Table or Fares without notice. They will not be liable for any loss, damage, injury or inconvenience that any passenger may sustain for any failure to maintain the service or for want of punctuality.

THE ROYAL MEWS, Norwich Avenue,
Bournemouth. Telephone **2264.**

(By Order) **W. W. GRAHAM,**
General Manager.

9th February, 1920.

The first journeys through the New Forest—and the 'Hants & Dorset' title was in use, well before it was officially adopted (see Chapter Four—a real start)

Road. This gave details of the three journeys in each direction made by just two buses based at Winchester and Lymington, which began running into Southampton on 23 and 28 February, respectively. The month of March did have its brighter side, however, for the company acquired the base essential to its establishment in the town; entering into an agreement with Councillor S. Tebbutt (who had properly abstained during the voting in committee, upon the granting of licences to the company), for the purchase of his premises in Shirley Road and small fleet of touring charabancs.

TRADE CARS

Tebbutt's contribution towards motoring in Southampton had been considerable. A keen pioneer driver (CR 2 and CR 4 were both registered in his name), he did much to encourage the use of motor vehicles, purchasing one of the earliest motor-van fleets for his main business venture, the 'Yacht Laundry'. After the Armistice in 1918, he noted that the pre-war charabanc operators had failed to re-establish themselves and decided to enter that field himself. He bought a second-hand Alldays & Onions charabanc called the 'Red Rover' and formed Trade Cars Ltd.

So that he might provide year round employment for his drivers, Tebbutt next acquired an ex-Army Halley 3-ton lorry and the property at the rear of his Villiers Road laundry—Durham House at 368 Shirley Road. The garden was converted into a suitable hard-standing area and a tyre press and other equipment were installed. Under a sub-contract from another local pioneer, Captain Reginald Keevil, a sombre winter's task was found for the Halley. One of the drivers, L. L. Honeybourne, DCM, recalls:

> We drove up to Morn Hill, about one and a half miles out of Winchester. There was a camp on the golf course and officers supervising the exhumation of American war casualties for shipment to The States. They put them in metal coffins and covered that with an outer case of polished wood. A brand new Stars & Stripes was then carefully folded over each and the whole lot boarded up into a packing case. Eight at a time were loaded on to

the Halley and we drove very slowly down to the American Remount Depot at Bassett Road, Swaythling. That's as far as we went: Keevil took them on to the docks from there.

Three other vehicles were added to the charabanc fleet and tours were advertised from Shirley Road, but the main pick-up point was Prospect Place Junction, beside West Park. All four were also licensed by Itchen Rural District Council for tours from Woolston.

The freehold of Durham House was secured on 18 May 1920 and the following month the Trade Cars licences also passed to Bournemouth & District Motor Services Ltd. Three drivers, a fitter, the maintenance staff of three, together with the office staff were transferred complete—and took charge of the Leyland saloons which were sent from Bournemouth.

The original Trade Cars staff rose to high places in their new employment: W. H. Willoughby, who had been manager, became branch manager for Hants & Dorset in Southampton, a post which he held for over twenty years. L. L. Honeybourne became first an inspector, then—in 1945—depot superintendent at Fareham, whilst another driver, George Pritchard, was appointed inspector at Bournemouth and Ringwood. On the maintenance side, Sid Warner was made general foreman of the Southampton Works and was still recruiting staff some five years later, whilst one of the original teenage mechanics Ivan 'Jim' Berry, retired from his post of general foreman in April 1971 with what must be the all-time record of service for any employee of Hants & Dorset (William Cox, who was still employed about Bournemouth Bus Station in his eighties, spent a large proportion of his service with W. W. Graham & Co). In their early days, the ex-Trade Cars mechanics were at the receiving end of some good-natured banter from company drivers. If a vehicle refused to start they would cry, 'Call out the gardeners, they'll sort it out'; a facetious reference to the mass of foliage which once graced the front of the premises and the additional duty of the younger mechanics to keep it tidy. Yet they quickly won respect by their apparent ability to perform the impossible with the limited number of vehicles available.

MAKING A START

Bournemouth & District still did not possess the necessary licences to operate Southampton-based vehicles on an advertised timetable, so the three new drivers were instructed to take the Leylands along the routes, without passengers, in order to publicise the service. This expensive charade eventually paid dividends, because when the licences were at last granted, the locals were clamouring to come aboard. The two Southampton-based buses then began running to Lymington and Winchester. At Lymington, passengers transferred to Bournemouth-based buses: through running only became possible when Southampton drivers had passed a Bournemouth Police driving test. Licences for further departures from Southampton were withheld until 15 July 1920. The Winchester service was then stepped up to nine journeys per day and a free hand was gained by the acquisition of the licence held by F. H. Bunce of Chandlersford. These two services operated from Southampton under the Bournemouth & District fleetname, although a few vehicles carried this beyond the renaming date until it was convenient for them to enter the workshop.

In August 1920, the Romsey service commenced running by way of Nursling, to be followed by another through Chilworth. But deliveries of new buses were still very slow and only five further Leyland 'G5's were registered in Southampton between July and December 1920. Yet the timetable case placed at the entrance to Sussex Road so many months earlier, began to fill out as the Southampton fleet gradually increased and each new arrival took its place in the omnibus rank beside Smith, Bradbeer & Co's corner drapery stores. Pushing out towards the north-east, a route through Swaythling and Botley to Bishops Waltham saw the company across the river Itchen. A few months later, in response to demand, the number of journeys per day had been raised to six and in 1922, three were extended to Droxford, East Meon and Petersfield, through the beautiful upper reaches of the

Page 87 (*above*) 'Gainst you wind up, be time for you to go'—Inspector George Felmingham of Gosport; (*right*) waiting to be 'wound up'—a Leyland TD1 open-topper

Page 88 The early Thirties look: (*above*) a low-loading Leyland LT5 'Lion' saloon; (*below*) a Leyland TD1 'Titan', one of Hants & Dorset's first fully enclosed double deckers

Meon Valley and terminating at the most easterly point served by the company. The last bus arrived at Petersfield Market at 9pm and was parked overnight, little more than a mile from the boundary with Sussex. At this stage, BAT's plan for such routes to link the South Coast with London must have seemed very close to fulfilment, for the capital lay a mere 53 miles away. But, in the event, only one more route to Petersfield (from Winchester) was established by Hants & Dorset and, as the managements of its sister companies began to change, so their areas became clearly delineated. Petersfield was destined to become the operational corner-stone for Hants & Dorset, Southdown and Aldershot & District.

TO PORTSMOUTH

In May 1921, a service through Botley and Wickham to the 'Crown Hotel', Fareham was pioneered, with three journeys per day; each taking 1½ hours to complete. Next, talks with Southdown Motor Services Ltd investigated the feasibility of a joint Southampton–Fareham–Portsmouth service: each company to handle the application for the other at their own end of the proposed route. On 28 November 1922, Portsmouth Corporation granted to Southdown's agent, Mr Bartlett, eleven drivers' and eleven conductors' licences for use by Hants & Dorset crews based upon Southampton. The 6d minimum fare ruling was applied in both towns and the total running time of the extended service was 1 hour 55 minutes, but an early morning newspaper special—known to the crews as the 'round the world trip'—travelled on a circuitous route which included Eastleigh, Winchester, Bishops Waltham, Fareham and Cosham—and vice versa for the Southdown vehicle. This led to the provision, the following year, of a joint Winchester–Portsmouth service with each company providing two return journeys per day: travelling time between terminal points, 2 hours 15 minutes. In 1925, Portsmouth Corporation relaxed the minimum-fare policy and both companies were able to charge penny fares between Victoria Hall and Air Balloon, Royal Hospital and North End, North End and Copsey's Siding,

Hilsea Post Office and Cosham, and Cosham to 1st Avenue, Wymering.

On the Southampton road, competition was met for a brief period in the shape of Henry Hodder's bus which left Portsmouth Dockyard's 'Unicorn Gate' and travelled out of town via Regent Street and Commercial Road. But the length of the route and the tolls which were imposed at Northam favoured the large capacity vehicles and this opposition ceased. Northam Bridge, together with its approach roads, had not yet become the property of Southampton Corporation (who later reduced and then dispensed with the toll) and a charge of 4s (20p) was made for an omnibus. On the outward journey from Southampton, the toll was taken at the bridge and on the inward, at Lances Hill; the conductor delving into his leather bag for the correct coinage. During 1922–3, some of the journeys were made via Swanwick and Titchfield, but these had been suspended the following year.

'Through running' between Southampton, Winchester and Portsmouth was a comparatively short-lived affair. In 1924 Hants & Dorset, having established itself at Gosport, had succeeded in pushing its area to the shores of Portsmouth Harbour. This left Southdown with two lengthy routes penetrating the territory of a sister company for, although the two were later to take on disparate characters as Hants & Dorset moved deeper into the fold of the Tilling organisation, the managements were at the time almost as close as they are today under the aegis of the National Bus Company. In order to give the smaller company an opportunity to consolidate its area, it was agreed that both would terminate their journeys at Fareham. Hants & Dorset acquired an office and waiting room at 12 West Street, the main thoroughfare of that town, and those passengers wishing to travel beyond Fareham, changed to the other company's bus. When, in February 1926, this came into effect, a new series of 'through tickets' was introduced—with the proviso that these tickets should be valid upon the day of issue only (a proviso that applied to all routes until 15 March 1927).

The withdrawal from Southampton and Winchester seems to have had little effect upon the fortunes of Southdown, for their

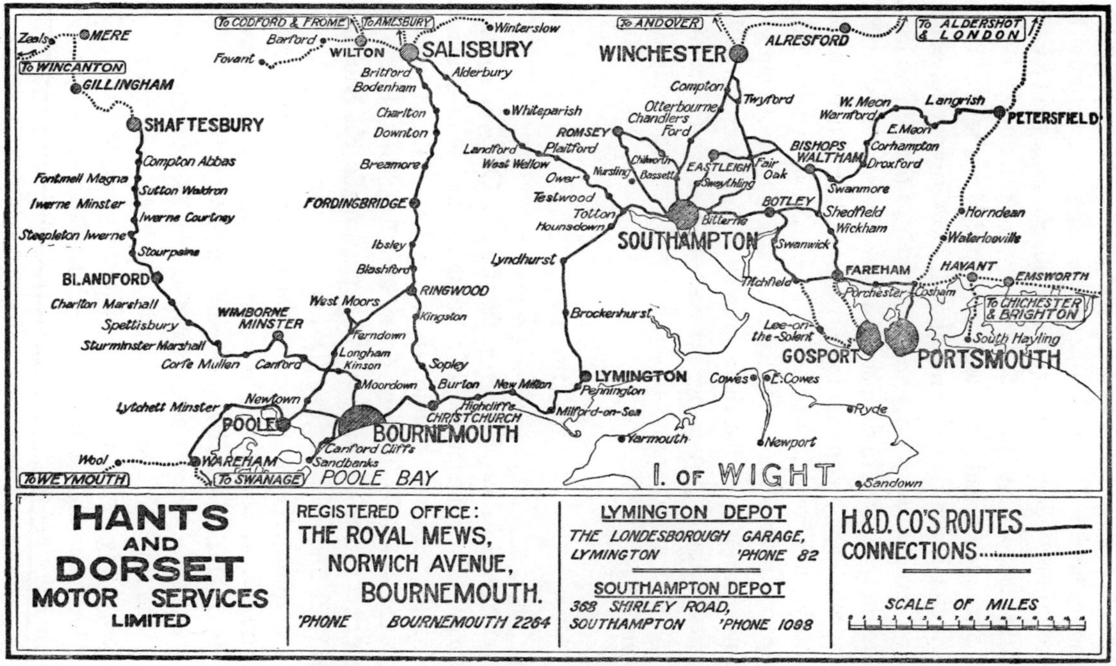

Route map for 1923, printed from the original block. There were services to Portsmouth, but none in the Gosport area

1926 profits broke all previous records, whilst Hants & Dorset's from Portsmouth seems to have benefitted the corporation tramways but little, for they suffered a loss of £18,000 during the following financial year and blamed unrestricted activity by private omnibus operators. There was probably more than a grain of truth in that: whilst Hants & Dorset were running to Portsmouth, Southdown had sixty vehicles available for service from that town alone, at a time when Hants & Dorset owned a grand total of 40 omnibuses and charabancs for use in their entire area.

It is unlikely that more than six Hants & Dorset buses carried plates entitling them to operate in Portsmouth, with a like number for Southdown in respect of Southampton. An interesting sidelight upon road transport in Portsmouth, at the time of Hants & Dorset's withdrawal, is that there were still omnibuses drawn by three horses abreast, running between Eastney and Hayling Ferry; 25 years after the first motor bus had been introduced to that town.

FILLING IN

A service to Salisbury began on Saturday, 1 October 1921. It was introduced to the public as a 'joint service' with Wilts & Dorset Motor Services Ltd, but whereas Wilts & Dorset (service No 4) went through Totton, Ower and Landford, Hants & Dorset's two return journeys per day were made via Nursling, Romsey and Sherfield English (taking 10 minutes longer, at 1 hour 55 minutes). This arrangement lasted precisely four weeks: the Romsey, Whiteparish, and Salisbury section was discontinued and Wilts & Dorset were left to provide the link between Southampton and Salisbury via Totton and Ower. Throughout 1922, they maintained two return journeys per day, with Hants & Dorset providing the occasional bus if demand made this worthwhile. There was then a complete withdrawal until 1925, when both companies began short journeys from their own end of the route. Conductor Sid Walker, known in his prime as 'the conductor that whistles and sings and makes us laugh', worked on this duty:

> We used to run through Totton and Testwood as far as 'The Vine' at Ower. The Wilts & Dorset bus met us in the forecourt and we'd swop passengers. Then they agreed to make it a joint operation and we went right through to Endless Street, Salisbury. Those were the days when conductors used to do favours, like taking orders for shopping or letting the old folk pay on the return journey, after they'd been in to get their pension. Parcels were our 'perks': we were allowed to charge a few pence for carrying them and share out the profits. But then they brought in the blue ticket system and we had to sign the waybill when we'd delivered the goods.

Hants & Dorset once operated a service from Southampton to Stockbridge. It opened on Monday, 28 May 1923, and its brief span has been recorded by Caleb Sutton of Regents Park, Southampton, in one of those unusually full diaries which are a transport historian's delight:

> I started on the Hants & Dorset in 1923. I was living in Stockbridge at the time and Sid Warner, the foreman at Southampton, came out on the Company motorbike to offer me a job as a conductor. They were starting a bus service between Stockbridge and Sussex Place, Southampton—via Kings Somborne and Romsey—and wanted to outstation a bus at Stockbridge. Well, I accepted the job and got £2 13s od (£2.65) per week. The service didn't pay though: it only ran that summer and on Sunday, 11 September it was withdrawn. 'Following day, I became a Southampton-based conductor learning the new route to Brook which had just started. I also did the No. 9 duty to Petersfield, the Lymington and Bournemouth run—and the 'round the world trip to Portsmouth!

The following year Caleb Sutton, a qualified turner and fitter, took his tools to the depot at Shirley Road, where he accepted a rise of 4s 6d (22½p) per week and began a career in the Central Workshops. He became foreman in 1946.

There now began a process of 'filling-in' the radial routes with shorter journeys. A new run to Marchwood, through the toll gate at Eling, covered part of the route worked many years before by an LSWR omnibus. Southampton-based buses also began operating from Eastleigh, although these later became the responsibility of the Winchester depot. Whilst the rural nature of such routes attracted many passengers, they nevertheless had their own special hazards: presupposing that the driver had successfully manoeuvred around the numerous farm waggons and animals, the tar barrels and steam rollers, there was always the dreaded overhanging tree. This placed baggage stowed on the roof rack at risk, and more than one conductor has told of leaving a push chair swinging from a branch. 'We'd stop the bus and back up until I could reach it from the top of the ladder and tie it back in place.' The majority of larger saloons were fitted with roof racks —reached from an eight-runged ladder at the rear of the bus— until the late thirties.

ADVERTISEMENTS

The elderly Leyland 'G5's had now been joined by three half-cab SG9s, a pair of 'GH7' double-deckers and several of the powerful new Leyland PLSC 1 'Lions'. The latter posed an unexpected problem for the conductors. All previous saloons had been fitted with rear entrances and they had become accustomed to keeping an avuncular eye on their passengers from the rear step. The new Leyland bodywork featured a front entrance—and the conductors found to their surprise that facing the passengers throughout the journey was an embarrassment. So thereafter, they turned and peered out of the front window, but—as one said—'A schoolmaster doesn't know what's going on in his class while he's writing on the blackboard!'

The open-topped GH7 had been put to work on several of the more heavily patronised routes from 1926 onwards. Instructions for driving them through the railway arch at Swaythling were drawn up:

> Drivers of open-top double deck omnibuses must slow down their vehicle immediately before proceeding under the bridge. Conductors must mount the top of the omnibus and caution passengers to remain seated during the passage of the vehicle under the bridge.

There is, of course, the tale of the unfortunate French visitor who was told to 'look out' and promptly obliged, but a corporation tram passing under the Bargate is also credited with this 'probable'. Many GH7s carried an advertisement for a Portsmouth brewery across the front of the top deck—as did most open-toppers later delivered—and one of these provided a legendary company tale. Until 1930, the advertisement simply named the brewery in white letters against a red background. Somewhere to the west of Southampton an inspector of the company, who lived opposite a bus stop, watched fascinated as an elderly lady refused to board several Hants & Dorset buses: there was no other operator working the route and all the buses were Southampton-bound. Curious, the inspector crossed the road and asked the now visibly weary lady why she had not boarded the buses which had stopped. To which she replied, 'I came out here on a BRICKWOODS bus. I always travel on BRICKWOODS buses because they are so friendly—and I intend going back on one!' It is said that this story of misplaced devotion reached the ears of William Graham at Bournemouth and that a request passed along the coast to Portsmouth, asking that the names of one or two beers might be included.

The introduction of double-deckers meant that selling advertising space could become company policy. Previously, all advertisements had been paper stickers attached to the interior of the windows. Customers now placed their orders in the hands of an agency, which produced the enamelled metal panels. These were brought to Southampton in the evenings; the agency employees working through the night, bolting them to the buses. Each vehicle which carried a full complement earned enough to pay its own maintenance costs. Towards the end of the twenties, the panels gave way to hand-painted inscriptions and for a short period practically every available space carried one. Apart from being aesthetically undesirable, this tended to confuse many more passengers than one old lady and, following the appointment of P. S. Pelling as chief engineer, advertisements were restricted to one upon each side panel, one below the rear window, a small strip above the rear window and a disc on the offside rear corner.

THE BATTLE OF LYNDHURST

The twelve routes being operated from Southampton and Eastleigh had been established without recourse to further acquisition of competitors' licences. Indeed, all had been progressing so smoothly that the provision of a 'tramway replacement' service with the company's three remaining charabancs, during the General Strike of May 1926, came as a welcome diversion for some of the crews: this was run between the Dock Gates in Canute Road and Shirley Tram Terminus, with appropriate stickers on the windscreens. That same summer, however, this calm was suddenly dispelled as a newcomer appeared on the road to Lyndhurst. Thus began a rivalry which was followed with great interest by the locals, who enjoyed a brief and hysterical period of rides at give-away prices.

Hants & Dorset had been running additional buses along the Lyndhurst route in order to cope with the growing number of Sotonians who seemed anxious to forget the troubles of strike-torn England with a walk in the New Forest. Only one other operator had been working the route—C. A. Croucher of Lyndhurst, whose service was geared towards the requirements of the villagers. Now he was to find himself sandwiched between the contestants in the ensuing battle.

'Jock' T. Cousin of Foundry Lane, Freemantle, trading as 'The Richmond' had pioneered a route from Southampton to Romsey via Ower with a fleet of revolutionary Lancia saloons. Although temperamental, the Lancia 'Pentaiota' was undoubtedly the fastest omnibus on the market and an ideal tool for an operator in a hurry. These then were the vehicles which he suddenly switched on to the Lyndhurst road, initially placing his departures between Hants & Dorset's. The company's reply to 'the intrusion' came in the form of some Morris-Commercial 'chasers' hastily despatched from Bournemouth. As mentioned earlier, these functioned satisfactorily only if the opposition were mediocre: the Lancias were far from that! The little Morrises bowling along on their narrow pneumatics were completely outclassed. They were quickly withdrawn and replaced with Leyland 'Lions'.

When the competition began, the return fare between Southampton and Lyndhurst was 2s (10p), whilst the single was 1s 3d (6p). This was soon amended to 1s 6d ($7\frac{1}{2}$p) return and 10d (4p) single. Cousin undercut this by twopence. Hants & Dorset did likewise. Down went the fares again, until the passengers turned this cut-throat business into outright comedy by refusing to board either vehicle: both green and yellow buses stood at the same stop, whilst customers bargained with the drivers—'How much are you charging today? Oh, well we'll get the other one then, he's charging twopence less.' As a result, some Sotonians rightly boast of having made the trip at the height of the season for 6d ($2\frac{1}{2}$p) return, or as little as 5d (2p) by purchasing a bundle of twelve tickets. With the 'Lions' beginning to make an impression, even if only by their seating capacity, Cousin purchased one to augment his own fleet and had it specially tuned for fast acceleration.

Competition from 'The Richmond' forced the introduction of rides at near give-away prices in 1927: this two-sided advertisement was carried in the windows of Southampton-based buses

Yet, at the end of the summer of 1927, as suddenly as it had all begun, the battle was over. Cousin sold his entire fleet and licences to Capt Reginald Keevil, to be incorporated into his 'Waterways & Docks Bus Company'. Hants & Dorset had won virtual freedom on the Lyndhurst road, and a few months later, most of the 'pirate' fleet joined the company's ranks, following the purchase of Keevil's licences. And when that happened, Hants & Dorset showed that they had learned well—they used the Lancias as 'chasers'.

To some extent, the generous use of open-toppers had helped the outcome of the Lyndhurst affair. The novelty of breezing along, dodging the leaves and enjoying the sunshine attracted many on to the upper deck. Accordingly, GH7s were now run in opposition to 'Greyhound Motor Coaches' on their service to West End and Moor Green. Originally the 'Woolston Queen', the proprietors Godfrey & Wilkins had moved their start point across the river, following the arrival of Southampton Corporation Tramways buses at Woolston. Hants & Dorset purchased Godfrey & Wilkins' service, together with three Lancias and a Thornycroft, in November 1927.

The purchase of the Waterways & Docks Bus Company—also completed that month—secured the monopoly of the Ower route to Romsey, a service between the Royal Pier and Southampton West Station, and increased traffic at the docks. (The fleet had included three ex-Southampton Corporation Thornycroft and one 'K class' London General double deckers, but these were not among the vehicles taken.) R. H. Keevil retained two Lancias and built up a new business named 'Holland Coaches', offering tours to the passengers of Dutch cruise ships berthed at the docks.

CONSOLIDATION IN THE FOREST

C. A. Croucher's 'Yellow Bus Service' was acquired in November 1928. His little Karrier omnibus was taken into the fleet and continued to operate to Lyndhurst. Part of the bargain which Croucher struck with the company was that the latter would promise not to raise the return fare between Southampton and Lyndhurst, Emery Down, Swan Green or Bank above 1s (5p). This the company honoured until the 1950 Finance Act forced a general fare increase some twenty-two years later. One of his drivers, Peter Piper, set up on his own at Emery Down after the sale, calling his one Chevrolet omnibus the 'Atlanta Bus Service', but Hants & Dorset purchased this also in December 1931.

As late as 1929, the pioneering spirit was abroad. Great reliance was still placed upon the initiative of the crews when new routes were established. Tom Jefferis's recollection of the first run to Fordingbridge is typical:

> I set out in a Leyland 'Lion' with George Arnold as my conductor, to start a new route to Fordingbridge. Prior to that, the service stopped at the Bell Hotel in Brook. It was a very foggy morning and I could just about see the side of the road—and to make matters worse, there were no passengers going and none coming back; well, not 'til Totton anyway. We found our way through Godshill and—eventually—down over the river into Fordingbridge, when we suddenly realised that nobody had told us where to stop. George was offering advice through the window behind me and I said we'd take the Damerham Road and look for a likely spot. So, we circled round and stopped where the road forks and decided that that was the terminus. When we got back, Inspector Honeybourne said, 'Where did you stop? Oh, right, we'll have a post put up there then,' and as far as I know, that's where it is today. It was always an honour to have driven the first bus to some new place, but I wasn't too sure about that one. It would have been nice to have had a few passengers.

Soon afterward, Tom Jefferis left, to become one of the better-known dealers in ex-company buses.

Another route branching away from Brook was acquired in January 1931, when the service operated by J. King & Sons' 'Kingson Motor Service' of Nomansland passed to the company. Two buses were purchased: one the comparatively rare AJS 'Pilot' half-cab saloon, which saw service with Hants & Dorset. A company bus has been stationed at Nomansland (on the border between Hampshire and Wiltshire) ever since that date. Other vehicles were outstationed at Lyndhurst, Ringwood, Romsey and

Bishops Waltham, to the east of Southampton; the latter being established at Rooke, Loader & Co's garage by S. W. Jefferis, who later became a director of Hutfield's Coaches of Gosport. When the Southampton depot assumed responsibility for the Calshot and Hythe Ferry route in June 1929, a dormy shed for double-deckers was erected at Calshot beside two bungalows, which were rented to the outstation crews. Through running did not begin on this route until the purchase of W. A. Woof's 'Premier Motor Service', by which time all the excitement generated by the staging of the Schneider Trophy races from Calshot Royal Air Force Station, was half forgotten and the base returned to its more mundane role of military seaplane station.

Inland, control of the area around Cadnam was secured in October 1936, when—shades of Sir Arthur Conan Doyle's 'White Company'—Mrs Sybil White, the proprietress of 'White Brothers Motor Service' of Minstead, decided to sell and become instead a taxi operator and parcel agent for the company.

THE OMNIBUS STATION

By the middle twenties, the Sussex Place stand had become inadequate and was abandoned in favour of another in Pound Tree Road. This, in turn, became swamped and plans for the construction of an omnibus station were set in motion. A row of shops in West Marlands Terrace was demolished and the new station completed as part of a development scheme for the Marlands. The administrative office block—which, together with the hard standing area, cost £37,500—was designed to harmonise with the classical façade of the Civic Centre opposite. It was opened on 24 January 1933, by Major-General Sir Reginald Ford, the chairman of the Traffic Commissioners, Southern Area, in a ceremony where bowler hats and local dignitaries were much in evidence. Originally, there was room for only sixteen omnibuses, but the standing area was almost immediately doubled, following the demolition of some houses at the north end of Birmingham Street. The roadside stands were forthwith abandoned.

WORKSHOPS AND GARAGES

For many years the Shirley Road premises served as both operational headquarters and workshop for the Eastern Area. In 1927 they were extended, and the days when lumps of glowing iron were placed across the floor, to keep the fitters warm, were over. Out too, went the clutch plate which was beaten with a hammer to signify 'time'. Then the building was extended through to Villiers Road, over ground once occupied by fruit trees and fowls; further space becoming available for the engineering section when the administrative offices were transferred to the new omnibus station.

Following the acquisition of Tourist Coaches' Excursion Department in 1935, it was decided that a new garage and work shop should be built upon the Bedford Place site. This was completed in 1938 and comprised tours offices, coach station, service area and a garage for over a hundred buses. The remainder of the operating staff was then transferred to this garage.

The Shirley Road Works was then reorganised to operate solely as the major overhaul depot for all company buses, a duty which it had previously performed with increasing difficulty. In its new form, it became one of the most efficient in the country, comprising engine and chassis shop, body shop and paint shop. With the equipment available and trained staff to match, almost every conceivable job could be tackled without resorting to outside contract. Unaccountably, however, Hants & Dorset was among the last to order self-starters for its buses and company drivers were winding-up and knocking little round holes in the backs of other buses with the starting handle, long after their municipal counterparts. It was many years before Shirley Road's little starter trolley (a Coventry flat-twin petrol engine on two wheels) could be dispensed with, but this became inevitable as an increasing number of buses was fitted with heavier five-cylinder Gardner oil engines.

SUMMARY OF ROUTE COMMENCEMENT DATES

(a)	(b)	(c)				
20	47	47	Southampton–Chandlers Ford–Winchester		Feb	1920
2	20	20	,,	–Lyndhurst–Lymington	,,	,,
14	36a	61	,,	–Nursling–Romsey	Aug	1920
21	48	48	,,	–Fair Oak–Winchester	Nov	1920
15	36b	62	,,	–Chilworth–Romsey	Dec	1920
—	—	—	,,	–Swaythling–Bishops Waltham	,,	,,
25	53	53	,,	–Botley–Fareham (1)	May	1921
—	—	61/6	,,	–Romsey–Salisbury (2)	Oct	1921
—	—	61/6	,,	– ,, –Winchester (3)	Nov	1921
19	51	50	,,	–Bishops Waltham–Petersfield	Oct	1922
—	—	—	,,	–Fareham–Cosham–Portsmouth (4)	Nov	1922
36	53a	54	,,	–Titchfield–Fareham	Oct	1922
—	—	—	,,	–Romsey–Stockbridge (5)	May	1923
16	39	40a	,,	–Totton–Brook	Aug	1923
17	34	58/9	,,	–Eling–Marchwood	Dec	1925
13	36	60	,,	–Ower–Romsey	Sept	1926
—	—	13a	,,	–Lyndhurst–Burley (6)	Nov	1926
17	34	58/9	,,	–Marchwood–Hythe	Sept	1927
—	39	39	,,	–Brook–Fordingbridge	Apr	1929
—	40	40a	,,	– ,, –Nomansland	Jan	1931

(1) Connections for Portsmouth by Southdown from Sept 1921
(2) Curtailed at Romsey Nov 1921
(3) ,, ,, ,, Mar 1922
(4) ,, ,, Fareham Feb 1926
(5) ,, ,, Romsey Sept 1923
(6) ,, ,, Lyndhurst Jan 1927

Route number series introduced: (a) 1927; (b) 1940; (c) 1946

CHAPTER SIX

TERRITORIAL DEVELOPMENT

LYMINGTON

LYMINGTON'S FIRST motor bus was a 17-seat, petrol-engined Thornycroft char-à-banc: it began working in July 1904 on the LSWR's road link between Lymington Station and Milford on Sea. Later, a pair of Clarkson steam buses were used between Lymington and Brockenhurst Railway Station, but in June 1918, George M. Backhurst & Co were approached by Lymington Council on the subject of the provision of motor omnibuses to meet specified trains at Brockenhurst, and who 'supported their application for petrol to the proper authority, as the firm appear to be ready to provide a real need for the town which has not been met by the LSWR Company'.

On 10 April 1919, the Finance Committee recommended that 'a Motor Bus Licence be granted to Lymington & District Motor Service Company Ltd, for a service to Boscome 5 or 6 times daily'. This company, under the management of E. A. Theadé, owned three omnibuses and a fleet of charabancs, which they operated from a garage constructed at the rear of the Londesborough Hotel in 1919. As mentioned earlier, Hants & Dorset eventually defeated this challenge by hiring a garage at New Street and covering every journey. Lymington & District's licences were acquired in November 1921 and the Londesborough Yard became the company's local depot (although the leasehold was not secured until 4 November 1925). H. F. Harrison was installed as manager and the depot's first duty was the supervision of the transfer of passengers between Bournemouth and

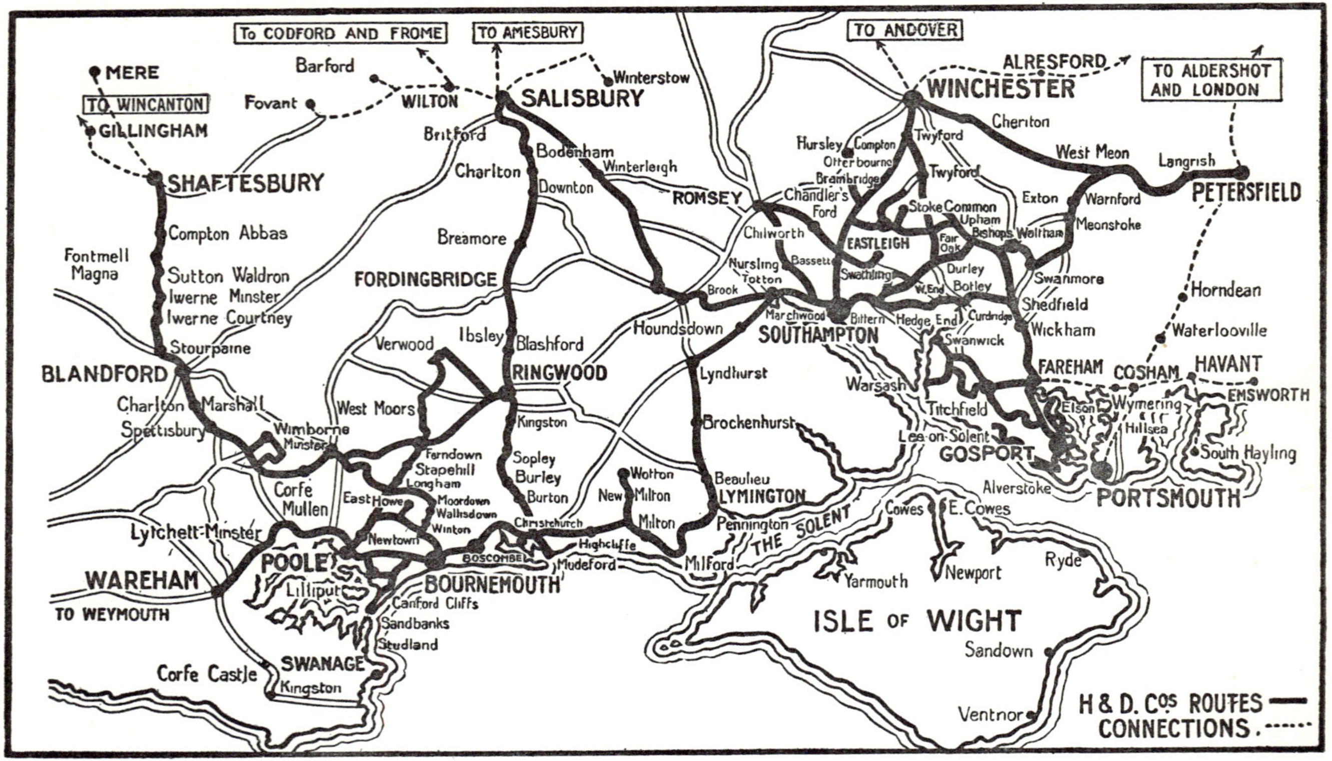

Official route map for 1926: Consolidation rather than expansion, particularly in the area to the east of Southampton. The route to Portsmouth had gone. (Beaulieu was misplaced)

Southampton-based vehicles. A service to Beaulieu, which went straight across Beaulieu Heath initially, began on 23 May 1925: shortly afterward it was being operated by the depot's only Morris 13-seater (No 148), at a time when tickets were so scarce that often none was available for issue. In April 1927, a pair of Leyland 'Leverets' took up the journey, which was extended to Hythe Ferry where connections with the steamboat service to Southampton were provided.

On Sundays, throughout the late twenties and thirties, local buses were timetabled to wait for the close of Matins at Christchurch Priory and Lymington Church. A similar 'personal touch' was evident when, in September 1932, Hants & Dorset began running over the original LSWR route between Lymington Town Station and Milford on Sea—and on to Keyhaven War Memorial. Passengers could ask to be taken direct to their homes in Milford at little extra cost, or telephone the Lymington depot and ask to be picked up at their door if they wished to catch a train. From June 1933, this feeder service was the preserve of 20-seat Leyland 'Cubs', which were much used at Lymington until World War II, when the Lymington Station journeys were suspended.

Acquisitions played a major role in the development of the depot. In August 1930, the Christchurch and New Milton service previously operated by Cyril Dawson was acquired, followed by Wootton to New Milton and Barton on Sea service of T. E. Dawes 'New Milton & District Motor Services'. The additional vehicles acquired were based at the Londesborough Yard. To provide a larger marshalling area, a butcher's shop and a row of cottages were purchased and demolished, whilst land already occupied was exchanged for an area containing some greenhouses. Thus a yard of suitable proportions was established, but for many years the buses continued to come in and out through a gap which was far too narrow for comfort.

The basic pattern of the Lymington-controlled services was almost complete following the transfer to the company of the Pennington, Sway and New Milton service of E. E. Gray's 'Oakleigh Motor Services', the Boldre, Pilley, Portmore and the Wainsford, Wootton and New Milton services of E. R. & E. M.

Whitren's 'Billie's Bus Service'; by February 1933. Heavier holiday traffic was reflected in the provision of a summer service to Pennington Cross and an overall increase elsewhere.

SUMMARY OF ROUTE COMMENCEMENT DATES

(a)	(b)	(c)		
2	20	20	Lymington–Lyndhurst–Southampton	Feb 1920
6	33	107	„ –Beaulieu	May 1925
6	33	107	„ – „ –Hythe Ferry	Apr 1927
6	33/4	—	„ –Hythe–Calshot	July 1927
—	22a	18	Christchurch–New Milton–Barton on Sea	Sept 1930
—	22	117	Wootton–New Milton–Barton Court	„ „
—	—	110	Lymington–Milford on Sea–Keyhaven	Sept 1932
—	24	112	„ –Boldre–Pilley–Portmore	Feb 1933
—	23	109	„ –Wainsford–Wootton–New Milton	„ „
—	—	110	Woodside–Lymington–Pennington	May 1935

Route number series introduced: (a) 1927; (b) 1940; (c) 1946

THE SWANAGE OUTSTATION

'The road to Swanage from Poole is narrow and twisty—and pot holey, owing to the char-a-banc service', so motorists were advised by *The Autocar* in August 1912. The offending chars-à-banc were owned by the Stevens Char-a-banc Company, based upon Messrs Stevens, Cottel, Pratt and Ball's Isle of Purbeck Garage in Swanage. They were green, 34hp Commer Cars, whose activities ceased in World War I.

In the early twenties, motor traffic was gradually re-established and stands for charabancs were allocated at Folly Knap (5), between the pier and the Royal Victoria Hotel Gardens (6) and at Shore Road (6). Among the operators represented were Dean & Barrett and Russell Parsons of the Station Garage, who both operated stage carriage services in the area.

Dean & Barrett began running a bus to Herston Cross in July

1924, a journey which involved a stiff climb out of Swanage. 'The Motor Tram passes the door of the Emmanuel Baptist Church, Howard Road, Swanage', an advertisement regularly informed the faithful. The vehicle—a passenger-carrying version of the refuse-collectors used by so many municipalities at the time —was a Shelvoke & Drewry 'Freighter', which featured tram-type controls and minute solid-tyred wheels. Originally brown and yellow, it offered places for 20 seated passengers with room for almost as many again standing. But, on 3 July 1926, the *Swanage Times & Directory* announced that:

> Owing to the complaints which have been made as to the noise of the moto-tram, the services to Herston via the King's Road and Newton have been suspended and the tram is now used exclusively on the New Swanage service. The cancellation has naturally caused inconvenience. One would have thought that the necessity for transport would have outweighed other considerations.

Mr C. S. Bennett, now superintendent of Hants & Dorset's Swanage depot, recalls that the 'moto-tram' was then acquired by Russell Parsons and put to work on the sea front. Mr Bennett was engaged to drive it between the pier and Parsons' 'Beach Cafe' (now the Ocean Bay), wooing the paddleboat passengers with promises of lobster and strawberry teas. During the off-peak season, it operated via Swanage Railway Station, New Swanage, Victoria Road and New Road, where on one occasion, a minor disaster occurred:

> The clutch used to slip sometimes. We had a rather amusing incident, when a rather stout lady who used to collect washing in one of those big baskets was on the bus. The clutch started slipping and it began to run away backwards. I steered to the side, but she made for the exit at the moment it hit the kerb—and she shot forward, straight into the basket. We had an awful job trying to get her out!

Three new Leyland PLSC 1 'Lions' arrived at the Royal Mews, Bournemouth in May 1926. They were intended—and indeed licensed for—a new route through Sandbanks to Swanage via the new link to be provided by the Bournemouth–Swanage Motor

Road & Ferry Company. But the steam ferry was almost immediately withdrawn with engine trouble and a defect in the prow-lifting gear. The General Strike did not hurry the project along either and the inauguration of the through service was therefore put back until April of the following year. By the autumn of 1927, four new Leyland PLSC 3 'Long Lions'—with places for 35 passengers—had taken over the duty, two of which were in fact canvas-roofed coaches, but since they were specifically employed upon a stage carriage service, this did not contravene the arrangement with Royal Blue, and for many years they proved the ideal vehicles for this beautiful seaside route.

Despite Hants & Dorset's arrangement with the proprietors of the newly opened ferry, their trial runs to Swanage were not unattended by a little local opposition. Some concern was expressed at the apparent lack of initiative on the part of those already operating to Studland. This stung one of them into negotiations with H. S. Rendell of Parkstone, to provide a joint service between Swanage and County Gates, but this failed when the necessary licences to complete the journey into Bournemouth were withheld.

The Swanage outstation and local town services were acquired when Russell Parsons decided to relinquish his service in favour of the company. Hants & Dorset purchased 3 Unic charabancs, a Ford T, the Shelvoke & Drewry and the Station Garage, whilst Parsons's manager, J. Hardy, became the local supervisor. The coaches were sold, but the 'Freighter' served for a further season.

A wooden office, rest and waiting room was then built opposite the pier and the Parsons fleet replaced with three Morris 13-seaters. The Herston Cross route quickly exposed the limitations of this type, however (as befitted his name, Hardy would clamp a telescope to his eye and will the distant bus to the hilltop), and a similar number of Leyland 'Leverets' took over in 1929. Within weeks of their arrival, business became so good that the crews volunteered to give up their rest days in order to cope with the Shell Bay traffic. Meanwhile, on the 'main road' service, the high chassis frames of the Leyland PLSC 'Lions' made light work of the ferry ramps, but the general introduction of low-loading saloons had, perforce, to be put back until a suitably designed vehicle became available. In 1935, four new Leyland LT5A 'Lions' arrived with 'ferry type' bodywork, specially cut away at an angle from the rear wheel—a feature which a proportion of company saloons have since incorporated.

When rough weather prevailed, the through service began running—by arrangement with the Southern National Omnibus Company—via Corfe Castle and Wareham, a facility which was put to good use for the last bus at night and, later, when the ferry service was suspended for the duration of the war and the coastline between Swanage and Studland was taken over by the military.

SUMMARY OF ROUTE COMMENCEMENT DATES

(a)	(b)	(c)		
12a	7	7	Swanage–Sandbanks–Bournemouth	Apr 1927
—	8	103	„ –Studland	Apr 1928
—	8a	104	„ –Herston Cross	„ „
—	—	105	„ –Durlston	„ „
—	9	104	„ –Sunnydale	„ „
—	—	106	„ –Sandbanks (or Wareham)–Poole	May 1950

Route number series introduced: (a) 1927; (b) 1940; (c) 1946

POOLE

Prior to 1928, all the company's operations within Poole Borough were based over the county border in Bournemouth. But a perusal of the Horse and Selection Committee records of Poole Council discloses that these services very nearly became the preserve of another high-powered operator and, bearing in mind the difficulties encountered in Bournemouth at the outset, if they had, it is extremely difficult to see just where 'Bournemouth & District' could have started.

First to be served by the railway and first—by a short head—with an electric tramways system, Poole gave qualified support for the establishment of a trolleybus service some twenty years before Bournemouth's was inaugurated (in May 1933). Founded in 1913, the Poole, Sandbanks & Westbourne Electric Car Company Ltd intended running trolleybuses along three routes not served by tramcars:

1. County Gates, The Avenue, Western Road, Canford Cliffs, Shore Road and the Haven Hotel, Sandbanks.
2. an alternative route along Ravine Road.
3. Sandbanks, Shore Road, Lilliput Hill Road, Sandbanks Road and Park Gates East.

The committee declared themselves willing to grant tentative permission, subject to the approval of the Board of Trade and with the most important proviso: 'that the company should be prepared to sell the undertaking as a going concern after a period of 15 years. Thus, Poole Corporation would have acquired a trolleybus undertaking in 1929—and might well have considered extending this form of traction over the Lower Parkstone route instead of agreeing to the substitution of Hants & Dorset buses when the trams were withdrawn. But in the event, when World War I commenced, the whole matter was dropped. The council instead invited Eugene Poulain to reinstate his service between Sandbanks and Park Gates East (qv) and both he and George Fox survived as omnibus operators.

When, in 1928, Poole granted licences to Hants & Dorset for the services through Lower Parkstone and Lilliput, it was decided to establish a depot in the town. A garage for four vehicles was built near the George Hotel, stocked with Leyland 'Lions' and Inspector Megson was sent from Bournemouth to supervise. One of the first tasks was the recovery of some lost territory.

Bournemouth & District's acquisition of the stage carriage service between County Gates, Sandbanks and Poole has been described earlier. After 1921, the latter had been allowed to lapse, as buses were pressed into service on newly opened routes in Hampshire. This proved fortuitous for one of the company's early rivals—and a most ingenious one at that. If anyone could be said to have given the fledgling company a run for its money, the honour must surely go to Miss L. Foott.

Driver and mechanic attached to the Headquarters Staff during World War I, the intrepid young lady arrived at Sandbanks after the Armistice, together with a Ford T presented to her by the Canadian Army and proceeded to build up a bus service with further Ford Ts specially lengthened into 10-seaters. Her spidery little buses ran at first to Park Gates and Poole—and then appeared at Parkstone and County Gates. Exercising her wit with gloriously inappropriate grandiloquence, the proprietress labelled each with the names Henry I, Henry II, etc, as far as Henry VIII—and then threw in his wives for good measure. An application to run camel-drawn wagonettes was turned down, but captured the imagination and affection of the locals, and revenue increased.

Their routes to the eastward now consolidated, Hants & Dorset became seriously concerned with the presence of this ever-growing fleet and sought to win back local support. Posters appeared throughout the area, exhorting the populace to 'patronise the green bus'. With characteristic adroitness, Miss Foott had her entire fleet through the workshops overnight, to emerge the following morning resplendent in bright green paint. Her supporters were not only delighted, they were also willing to lend a hand: on one occasion, a Ford T was pinned nose-to-tail at the stand as the time to depart approached, but the vehicle proved so light, that passengers and bystanders pitched in and pulled it out sideways.

Eventually, however, the weight of the opposition rendered further operation from Sandbanks unprofitable and Hants & Dorset regained the licences for the Poole service in March 1929. Unwilling to concede all, Miss Foott obtained exclusive rights for a service from Parkstone to a gypsy encampment on gorse-covered heathland. Over the years, extensive estates grew where once the caravans stood and Mrs Dingwall-Foott's 'Rossmore Bus Service' became the only one in Poole not operated by Hants & Dorset.

The well-documented contest with the fleet of Foott tends to overshadow another rival on the County Gates route, H. S. Rendell, who ran a pair of 14-seat buses. After giving up his licence in May 1929, he concentrated upon excursion work and his business (Cosy Coaches) still operates from Parkstone.

WAREHAM AND BERE REGIS

In 1923, the company started operating between Bournemouth and the Red Lion, Wareham, via Lytchett and Holton Heath. The fares were 1s 9d (9p) single and 3s (15p) return. Two journeys per day were provided between the Red Lion and Swanage by the National Omnibus & Transport Company Ltd (Southern National from January 1929), but it was not until National had acquired the licence of Nicholl's Langton–Matravers to Swanage service and installed him as their local supervisor, that fully integrated journeys were introduced, running through Langton-Matravers and Corfe Castle. This connection came into operation on 1 June 1929. From that day also, National provided four connecting departures for Wool, Osmington and Weymouth—with through fares from Bournemouth at 3s 6d (17½p) single and 6s (30p) return.

Next, Hants & Dorset reappeared on the road to Dorchester, following the acquisition of George Vacher's 'Bere Regis Motor Service'. Vacher had taken over the licences of the Weymouth Motor Company Ltd, in respect of a Monday, Wednesday and Saturday service between Weymouth and Bournemouth. He cut short the journeys at Dorchester and Poole, introduced a Tuesday service and another which ran through to Bournemouth on Fridays. Since Vacher was a personal friend of William Graham, his vehicles were granted terminal facilities at The Royal Mews. Fred Hann—later the landlord of the Rising Sun at Wimborne—and Reginald Toop were drivers for Bere Regis Motor Service, but whilst Hann became a driver for Hants & Dorset, the latter broke away to form his own business, 'Bere Regis & District Motor Services'. Vacher's other services were run mostly on market days: Bere Regis to Blandford via Almer on Fridays (Thursdays later), Bere Regis to Wimborne via Almer on Tuesdays, Bere Regis to Wareham via Lane End on Thursdays and via

Bloxworth and Morden on Saturdays. These, together with the garage in North Street, Bere Regis and the vehicles—which were operated briefly, but neither repainted nor numbered—were purchased in August 1930. George Vacher was placed in charge of the company's services in the area, the premises being known as the Bere Regis depot until World War II. His buses were replaced by the company's own Chevrolet LQ saloons, until these were in turn ousted by Dennis 'Ace' saloons in 1934.

Since Vacher had terminated his westward journeys at Dorchester, an agreement was reached with Southern National whereby a through service between Bournemouth and Weymouth permitted the vehicles of both companies to run over the entire length of the route. Joint-running began in September 1930, with the terminal point the King's Statue in Weymouth. The following year, Hants & Dorset were granted running rights beyond this stage to Southwell on the Isle of Portland—the most southerly point ever served by the company—but at the close of the 1933 season, this section became the exclusive preserve of Southern National.

TRAMWAY REPLACEMENT (1)

The Brush Electrical Engineering Company's tender for the construction of the Parkstone Light Railway extension had been £26,167 18s 3d and—in February 1906—the Board of Trade had permitted the Borough of Poole to borrow £29,063 for a period of thirty years, to pay for it. Yet, seven years before the deadline, it was the turn of the lessees, Bournemouth Corporation Tramways Department, to invite tenders for taking up this 2½ mile track. Hants & Dorset were thus able to announce that, from 6 January 1929:

> By arrangement with the respective Corporations, a Direct Service of Double Decked Omnibuses will be operated between
> BOURNEMOUTH AND POOLE
> The route will be to and from the Omnibus Stand, Avenue Road, Bournemouth, round the Square and then via Poole Road

to County Gates, Lindsay Road, Archway Road, Bournemouth Road, Parkstone to the Library, High Street, Poole.

Week Days, leaving Bournemouth at 5-50, 6-0, 6-20, 6-40, 7-0 a.m., and then every 10 minutes up to and including 11-30 p.m.

Sundays, leaving Bournemouth at 10-0 a.m., and then every 10 minutes up to and including 11-30 p.m.

Week Days, leaving Poole at 5-50, 6-0, 6-20, 6-40 a.m., and then every 10 minutes up to and including 11-20 p.m.

Sundays, leaving Poole at 10 a.m., and then every 10 minutes up to and including 11–20 p.m.

This service is duplicated during Busy Periods; 8 a.m. to 9 a.m., and 2 p.m. to 6 p.m.

CONDITIONS OF SERVICE

Passengers are most particularly requested to note that the conditions relating to this service are:– that no persons can be carried on the above time-tabled omnibus who wish to COMMENCE and FINISH their journey in the Borough of Bournemouth. Passengers can be picked up en route for points Outside the Borough, but the first stop on the outward journey from Bournemouth at which passengers will be allowed to ALIGHT will be at the Omnibus Stand, County Gates, in the Borough of Poole; passengers coming into Bournemouth from outside the Borough can alight at any of the official stopping places.

STOPPING PLACES

In the Borough of Bournemouth are:– The Omnibus Stand, Avenue Road, near the Square; St. Michael's Church; West Station Entrance, (viz., on the Bournemouth side of the Hospital on the outward journey, and opposite the Hospital on the inward.) and from there direct to the County Gates Stand. In the Borough of Poole the stopping places are:– County Gates, Corner of Lindsay Road and Leicester Road; Corner of Archway Road and Penn Hill Avenue; Archway Road; and from there to Poole the stops recently used by the Trams.

POOLE AND BOURNEMOUTH FARES

For the first stage out of Bournemouth and the last stage into Bournemouth, viz., between Bournemouth and County Gates, the fare will be 2d. between County Gates and Poole, intermediate Fares on similar stages to the previous Tram Fares will be charged.

The Through Fare between Bournemouth and Poole and vice-versa will be 5d.

Workmen's and Children's Fares similar to those previously in operation.

Poole.					
1	Park Gates.				
2	1	St. Osmund's Church.			
3	2	1	St. Aldhelm's Church.		
4	3	2	1	County Gates.	
5	4	3	2	1	Bournemouth Square.

SPECIAL NOTICE

Omnibuses leaving Poole at 10, 30, and 50 minutes Past the Hour proceed via Longfleet. Also on the return journey, leaving Bournemouth at the Hour, 20 minutes and 40 minutes Past the Hour.

With the co-operation of the council, the company now ran from the George Hotel to Upton via Oakdale and to Corfe Mullen via Broadstone, extending this into an hourly service for Wimborne Square in July 1930. This brought the vehicles into direct competition with 'Poole & District Motor Services', owned by Russett Brothers and H. Venner of Newtown. During their four years of operation, they had built up a loosely connected string of services with a small, but impressive, collection of maroon and white buses. Hants & Dorset acquired the vehicles and the goodwill of the following services in September 1930: Upton–Newtown; Poole–Corfe Mullen–Wimborne; Wimborne–Colehill and Wimborne–Holt–Woodlands.

This increased traffic led—in January 1932—to the opening of a new garage and office in Towngate Street, the Wimborne Road premises becoming a parcel office.

TRAMWAY REPLACEMENT (2)

One of the most significant events in the company's history took place in September 1934. This was an agreement with Poole Council which led to the total substitution, some nine months later, of Hants & Dorset's petrol-powered buses for trams within the borough. As mentioned earlier, Bournemouth Corporation were responsible for the running of tramcars from Christchurch in the east to Poole Railway Station in the west—and in the case of the latter, over tracks owned by Poole Corporation. Ownership of the tramlines within Poole had been established in June 1905 and Bournemouth Corporation Tramways Department had been granted accordingly, a thirty-year lease to run their electric cars over the tracks. This arrangement was now due for renewal—or termination—at a time when tramways generally were being viewed with increasing disfavour. Naturally, a line of such length was a prestige matter—to say nothing of its remunerative value—for the operating tramways department, whose plans for the substitution of trolleybuses began to pale in the light of the negotiations between Poole and Hants & Dorset Motor Services Ltd.

The outcome of the original meeting was not disclosed until a meeting of all interested parties had taken place in London the following month. On 24 November 1934, it was made public with the following announcement:

SALE OF LIGHT RAILWAYS

> ... The Corporation shall sell and the Company [Hants & Dorset Motor Services Ltd] shall purchase for the sum of £75,000 the undertaking authorised by the Poole & District Light Railway Order of 1899, including the Light Railways constructed under the provisions of the said order, and the Tram Shed and Depot owned by the Corporation and used in connection with the said Light Railways.

At the eleventh hour, following a conference between Bournemouth Corporation, Poole Corporation and the Ministry of Transport, Hants & Dorset withdrew their application for the necessary licences and Poole re-opened talks with Bournemouth on the subject of trolleybuses. But, on 9 December 1934, Poole confirmed that the Transport Committee had been authorised to make an agreement with Hants & Dorset and to support the Parliamentary Bill which the company was to promote. Reluctant to believe that their cause was lost, Bournemouth were still seeking powers to operate trolleybuses in Poole as late as March of the following year. However, Poole were now determined to complete arrangements with Hants & Dorset and Bournemouth Corporation's last tram ran over Poole borough's tracks on 7 June 1935. The following day, a new fleet of Hants & Dorset double deckers took over the Parkstone Road, North Road and Ashley Road section previously operated by trams.

The Leyland 'Titans' specially ordered for these duties were fitted with the Leyland Torque Converter—a device costing £90, which dispensed with the usual gearbox: there was no gear changing—the driver accelerated the bus by opening the throttle and retarded it with the brakes. He could even permit it to run backwards downhill, gradually bring it to a standstill and move forward by use of the accelerator alone, without the slightest jerk. It was a bus which an ex-tram driver could be taught to drive with little difficulty.

Hants & Dorset took possession of the tram shed in Ashley Road and this became the Parkstone depot. Also, the company agreed to pay the borough of Poole a small percentage of the profits received from the carriage of passengers over the ex-tram routes and make a large contribution towards the cost of taking up the tramlines. The £75,000 'purchase fee' in effect bought 40 years' right of operation until 31 December 1975. (As prescribed, it was reviewed on 31 December 1957 and allowed to proceed.) This arrangement, together with that made with Bournemouth Corporation on 24 June 1935, was scheduled as part of the Poole Road Transport Act, 1935.

A series of carefully interconnected services was then developed and worked in the borough. Several road-rail interavailability routes were introduced and—as a pleasant personal touch—late omnibuses from Poole waited for the close of the Regent Theatre. In this quarter particularly, the company won high praise for the efficient manner with which they operated what was, in effect, a replacement municipal service.

SUMMARY OF ROUTE COMMENCEMENT DATES

(a)	(b)	(c)		
12	7	7	County Gates–Canford Cliffs–Sandbanks	Aug 1918
—	27	32	Poole–Park Gates–Sandbanks	May 1919
—	11	11	„ –Bere Regis–Dorchester	Oct 1920
11	10	89	(Bournemouth)–Poole–Wareham	May 1923
—	15	33/4	Hamworthy–Poole–Newtown	Mar 1927
—	13	23	Wallisdown–Branksome	June 1928
—	—	31	Poole–Lilliput–County Gates	„ „
—	2	2	„ –Lower Parkstone–County Gates	„ „
—	25	22	„ –Broadstone–Corfe Mullen	Feb 1929
—	25	22	„ –Corfe Mullen–Wimborne	Aug 1930
—	11	11	(Bournemouth)–Poole–Weymouth	Sept 1930
—	1/5	1/5	Five tramway replacement routes	Jun 1935

Route number series introduced: (a) 1927; (b) 1940; (c) 1946

GOSPORT & FAREHAM

The horse-drawn omnibus had arrived in Gosport by 1859, for White's *Gazetteer* mentions a service between the LSWR station and the Floating Bridge—a journey of some fourteen hundred yards—with the times arranged to suit the arrival and departure of the trains.

Twenty years later, the Provincial Tramways Company—already operating in Portsmouth—obtained permission to lay tracks from the Hard to Brockhurst, and from 1882, horse-drawn tramcars began to capture the railhead traffic. But, as was the case in Bournemouth, the motor omnibus made its debut before the electric tramcar: Arthur Julian, who had introduced motor wagonettes to the streets of Portsmouth in 1899, founded 'The Portsmouth & Gosport Motor Omnibus Company' in 1901 and an inaugural run to Fareham had been made on 4 January of the following year.

When control of the tramways on the Portsmouth side of the harbour passed to the corporation, Provincial obtained powers to extend their Gosport system to Fareham and, running under the title 'Gosport & Fareham Tramways Company', the first cars powered by electricity started in 1906. Four years later, Provincial were granted powers to operate motor buses throughout the triangular area bounded by Haslar, Wickham and the river Hamble. Three main routes were introduced: Gosport Ferry to Wickham via Fareham; Gosport Ferry to the Red Lion, Lower Swanwick via Brockhurst, Titchfield and Sarisbury Green—and a summer service between Gosport and Lee-on-Solent Pier. Yet, by the early twenties, the management had come to view the performance of motors with some disfavour; the trams having shown handsome profits because of the para-military nature of the local traffic—and this boom had continued beyond the war years. Provincial therefore agreed to the setting up of bus services by a handful of local operators—and two of these are of particular note: Tutt & Sons' 'Enterprise' and H. W. Smith's 'Yellow Motor Service'.

Both firms had begun by hiring out carriages and horse chars-à-banc (from stables in North Street and Beach Street respectively) and had turned to mechanical power in 1920. The Enterprise fleet was a mixed bag of Daimler, Dennis and Thornycroft charabancs and single decks, whilst an AEC and another Thornycroft were fitted with open-topped double-deck bodies. Enterprise took over Provincial's Wickham service and extended it to Swanmore and Bishop's Waltham. To this was added a route from Gosport Hard to Fareham and then on to Titchfield, Locksheath and Warsash—and a third from the Hard to Hardway and Elson. Meanwhile, Provincial persevered with their service to Lower Swanwick, their pale turquoise Thornycroft usually passing the maroon and cream Enterprise double-decker—southbound for Warsash—in Titchfield Square.

The Yellow Motor fleet originally comprised three Garford 20cwt trucks (rebuilt with 20-seat bus bodies), which were permitted to run over the Provincial route between the Hard and Lee-on-Solent. Here, the gravel surface of Gomer Lane and Military Road fractured their wooden wheels so often, that H. W. Smith obtained from the CRE Gosport a permit which enabled bus operators to make good the roads at their own expense—and this the crews were expected to carry out, as well as their normal duties. The Garfords were eventually superseded by a mixed fleet of Daimler charabancs and single-decked buses.

Tutt's services and ten of their vehicles were acquired by Hants & Dorset on 28 July 1924. On 1 September, Provincial relinquished their right to the Lower Swanwick route, and the transfer of the goodwill and seven vehicles from H. W. Smith's Lee-on-Solent service on the 29th, saw Hants & Dorset well established on the western shore of Portsmouth Harbour. An area office was opened in the Market House, opposite the Hard and buses from both acquired fleets continued in daily use until replacements were available—which turned out to be 'Charabuses'. Tutt's depot in Brockhurst Road—a refurbished aeroplane hangar—was utilised at first, but when Leyland 'GH7' open-toppers arrived, a garage with exceptionally high doors was purchased. On the sea front in Beach Street, it was previously owned by a company manufacturing hollow-spars for sailing yachts. And Father Neptune must have been somewhat displeased by its loss, for within weeks of its placement beneath the surface of the yard, the large capacity fuel tank fractured and over one hundred gallons of petrol sailed off to sea on the falling tide.

From the ranks of the Yellow Motor Service, came one of the best-known characters of Hants & Dorset's eastern area. George Felmingham, inspector extraordinary, conducted operations at the Hard and Clarence Square with a panache that was both efficient and entertaining. A smallish man with ruddy complexion and a Somerset accent, he'd a half-hunter nestling in his waistcoat pocket, another watch in the depths of his company greatcoat and a whistle which he was by no means reluctant to blow. Crews were summoned from 'the Dive'—a tea and sandwich bar beneath the company office—with the words, 'Gainst you wind up, be time for you to go', whilst venturesome drivers were admonished with such lines as: 'Next time I see you driftin' no-hands roun' the tramlines in Forton Road, it'll be the sack for you my lad!' Firm, but full of fun and an endless supply of jokes, he is remembered with affection by numerous senior busmen.

In the twenties, Hants & Dorset relinquished two services to

Page 121 Brush-bodied Leylands: (*above*) two LT5A 'Lions' disembark from the Bournemouth–Swanage Motor Road & Ferry Co's No 1 Ferry; (*below*) one of the torque-converter 'Titans' purchased for the Poole–Bournemouth tramway replacement service

Page 122 One of the first Beadle-bodied Leyland TS7 Tiger observation coaches, in Hants & Dorset's version of 'Royal Blue' livery—dark blue and turquoise

(*above*) 1936 period piece: 4 Tigers in 'Royal Blue' livery and the brand new *Queen Mary* at Southampton; (*below*) after the 1936 season, a cleverly proportioned green and cream livery replaced the original

the resurgent motor buses of Provincial: the Hardway and Elson service, handed over in 1926 and the Gosport Ferry to Alverstoke route acquired from J. R. Anderson's 'Blue Motors' in July 1929 —and which Hants & Dorset had operated for one day only.

The Gosport depot's pattern of development was complete, but from the day of its inception in 1924, it had assumed responsibility for traffic throughout the original 'Provincial' area. By purchasing the goodwill of Enterprise, the company had inherited one of its rivals—the Warsash & Fareham District Bus Service.

C. R. Fuger of Warsash had started after World War I with a 10-seater Studebaker on a complicated route which took in Warsash, Sarisbury Green and the Red Lion, Lower Swanwick (a section also operated by the Woolston, Bursledon & District Motor Service). It then backtracked, unopposed, through Sarisbury Green to Park Gate—then to Segensworth, Hill Park, Gudgeheath Lane and Fareham, where it stood nose-to-tail with a motley collection of small buses in the middle of West Street. The contest between Tutt and Fuger took place on the latter's second service to Fareham via Fleet End and Titchfield. Whilst Fuger ran via Park Gate—affording a link with his other service—Enterprise went via Church Road, direct to Locksheath; the route which Hants & Dorset were to inherit. The locals near Warsash and Locksheath tended to support Fuger, both by their custom and vocal effort, whilst the opposition were greeted with unsolicited advice. Farther east, Tutt's larger vehicles normally did the better business.

So, with a praiseworthy lack of colour prejudice, the good folk of Warsash and Locksheath greeted the Company's green buses with exactly the same banter afforded the red Enterprise vehicles. As one local puts it: 'They were about as welcome as a Saints supporter at Fratton Park, but it was all good natured stuff really.' (A reference to Southampton Football Club and Portsmouth's club ground, respectively.) Thus began a six-year contest which ended only after the involvement of Hants & Dorset's cruiserweight neighbour, Southdown Motor Services Ltd.

Until April 1926, an unwritten *modus vivendi* was honoured by both contestants. Then, following the acquisition of the Woolston,

Bursledon & District Motor Service's route between Warsash and Bursledon Toll Bridge (dealt with later), Hants & Dorset set out to gain exclusive rights in the area. Company buses for the Bursledon service were crewed from Gosport, some ten miles away—and Len Miller, a conductor who retired in 1963 after thirty-nine years' service, used to ride pillion behind his driver on a Hants & Dorset motorcycle, in order to take over the duty at Warsash. Clearly, some infilling was necessary.

In 1926, Fuger bought himself a Guy AB, solid tyred, but of low configuration—and its performance was at first sadly underestimated by the company, as S. W. Jefferis recalled:

> Fuger had an old Guy single decker and Hants & Dorset sent up one of their little Morris 'chasers' to run against it. Well, that Guy was a darned sight faster than they realised and the Morris couldn't touch it! After a few weeks' futile chasing, they sent a Leyland 'Leveret' instead; but it wasn't until they'd acquired some second-hand Lancias the following year, that any impression was made. To some extent, they can thank the drivers for that too, and I'll explain why: each time the six cylinder model went in for service, the foreman in charge used to regulate the flow of petrol by inserting standard jets. However, the drivers used to enter somewhat further into the spirit of the chase than was officially intended, because they'd dismantle the carburettor and push a needle through the aperture. Result—a very fast Lancia indeed!

Two Daimler 'CC' double-deckers with open tops also ran between Gosport and Warsash in late 1927, and Ernest Sandom recalls piloting one of these—with its completely open and screenless driving position—through a hail of well-aimed turf near the Sluice at Titchfield: he'd committed the unpardonable sin of transferring his employment from the local 'blue bus' to the company. From April 1927, additional buses were sent to Warsash on a more direct route via Stubbington and new departures made from Fareham. By 1929, the first shots in a price-war had been fired; the fares dropping in penny lots.

At this point, Fuger undertook a little research and discovered that a large proportion of his passengers went on to Portsmouth from Fareham in vehicles provided by Southdown Motor Services Ltd. He therefore purchased a fleet of five 20-seat Dennis buses and acquired licences to operate them beyond Fareham to Cosham and Portsmouth's Victoria Hall. Southdown, who had just run-in a fleet of Tilling-Stevens petrol electrics along the same road, watched with some disbelief as this unexpected competitor proceeded to run a total of twenty-eight journeys per day at half-hourly intervals (against forty-nine between Southsea and Fareham by Southdown). A bold throw indeed, but it was not a propitious moment to tackle a giant considerably larger than the one already engaged—particularly when the two were closely related (both Hants & Dorset and Southdown were controlled by BAT at the time). Like the chess player who advances before castling, Fuger was manifestly unprepared for the retaliatory action which this move precipitated. As 1929 drew to a close, Southdown purchased an old strawberry-packing station at Fleet End near Warsash and turned it into a dormy shed for two Leyland 'Titan' double deckers. Hants & Dorset then withdrew from the route, maintaining their title by the slenderest of threads —one journey each way on Wednesdays, Saturdays and Sundays, and that between Gosport and Stubbington to Warsash. Southdown then commenced operating thirty-two return journeys per day over the entire route of some fifteen miles, with buses capable of shifting over fifty passengers apiece. At the same time, the fares inherited from Hants & Dorset were at a low of 4d single and 6d return. No small operator could withstand competition of this kind for more than a few weeks—and the Warsash & Fareham District Bus Service duly capitulated on 1 May 1930.

Hants & Dorset purchased Fuger's vehicles and a daily express service he had operated from Warsash to London. Since the agreement with Royal Blue was still in force, Hants & Dorset were obliged to transfer this to Southdown, who eventually merged it with an express service acquired from 'Perseverance' of Gosport.

Turning their faces from the wall, Hants & Dorset reappeared in force on the Warsash route and joint-working west of Fareham was introduced: one Southdown and two Hants & Dorset buses per hour operating a rearranged timetable, with a change of vehicles at Fareham on the latter. Southdown retained their dormy shed at Fleet End and a stake in a route which extends 10 miles to the west of the demarcation line previously agreed upon in 1926.

HANTS & DORSET FARES TO TITCHFIELD AND WARSASH

Date	*Fareham to:*	*Single*		*Return*
June 1928	Titchfield	3d		5d
	Warsash	6d		10d
April 1929	Titchfield	2d		3d
	Warsash	4d		6d
June 1930	Titchfield	3d	*	4d
	Warsash	6d	*	10d

* These fares remained unaltered for the next 20 years, both companies' return tickets being accepted for cancellation upon the other's buses.

Although Hants & Dorset later came under the control of the Tilling Group, the joint running continued. (In recent times, a close managerial relationship has been re-established following the formation of the National Bus Company; shades of the past being revived in January 1969, when as a mutual convenience, all Hants & Dorset's Sunday journeys to Warsash from Fareham were withdrawn in favour of Southdown.)

In May 1930, an hourly service from Fareham to Bursledon started, which ran through Titchfield, Locksheath and Park Gate, connecting at the toll bridge with buses for Woolston and co-ordinating with the Catisfield and Segensworth journeys acquired from Fuger. It was also the year that the Southern Railway Company announced their decision to close the Solent Railway—a single line track between Fort Brockhurst and Lee-on-Solent, which terminated just short of the pier. Replacement Hants & Dorset buses began meeting the trains at Fareham Station in January 1931 and running to Lee via the now-closed Milvil Lane.

It had been realised some years previously that Fareham had become the natural co-axial point of the area: the geographical position of Gosport resulting in too much dead mileage. Realised, too, that the little office beside the Kings Arms at the Portsmouth end of Fareham's West Street had served its purpose, and that a large garage and bus station should be erected. The choice of site fell upon two properties at the junction of West and Portland Streets. One of these—an early Georgian house—excited the protective instincts of several townsfolk anxious to preserve a link with the writer William Thackeray. But this was a somewhat tenuous link: it was not Thackeray's birthplace; he had merely spent some childhood holidays there—and since he did not return after the age of fourteen, it is hardly likely that any of his essays were formulated in the house.

Controversy aside, the bus station in its original form was constructed to grant covered stowage to sixteen buses, with room for four at the passenger loading bays. There was an entrance to the marshalling area from West Street, through which Southdown buses from Portsmouth gained access to the bays on the east side, whilst Hants & Dorset's entered from Portland Street through a gap between the Southdown bays and the garage, coming to a halt on the opposite side. The premises were completed in July 1931—and since that date, the affairs of both Gosport and Fareham depots have been administered from the West Street bus station.

Two further acquisitions completed the pattern of the route structure extant today—E. H. Moore's buses, which once traded as the 'Solent View Service', and Shirrell Motor Services, the goodwill of both being transferred in February 1932. E. H. Moore—also a parcel agent for the Company—operated a fleet of small-capacity buses between Fareham, Hill Head and Lee. When he decided to sell, Hants & Dorset re-gained territory vacated in 1925—the road between Stubbington and Hill Head. The company had already obtained licences to run through Shirrell Heath, however, and had used the 'chaser' technique in opposition to Shirrell Motor Services. W. G. Butcher and W. R. Gamblin, the erstwhile owners, recall the competitive days with some amusement—indeed, a tacit and gentlemanly understanding seemed to be in force:

Once, our bus got a puncture right outside the garage. Well, we ran it onto the forecourt to put on a Stepney wheel and sent a lad up the road on his bike to where the Hants & Dorset had come to a halt. 'What's up then?' asked the driver. 'We're putting a new tyre on,' said the lad. 'Oh, all right then, I'll wait,' said the driver. We were all local chaps, you see!

Butcher & Gamblin's Shirrell Motor Service ran between Bishops Waltham, Fareham and Lee: they were the last of the numerous independents who once operated to Lee-on-Solent from Fareham.

SUMMARY OF ROUTE COMMENCEMENT DATES

(a)	(b)	(c)		
—	—	—	Fareham–Cosham–Portsmouth*	Nov 1922
24	54	69	Gosport–Fareham–Bishops Waltham	Jul 1924
32	62	77	,, – ,, –Warsash	,, ,,
—	—	—	,, –Hardway–Elson*	,, ,,
33	58	79	,, –Titchfield–Lower Swanwick	Sept 1924
34	60	72	,, –Browndown–Lee on Solent	,, ,,
—	—	72a	,, –Lee on Solent–Hill Head	,, ,,
—	64	79a	Warsash–Sarisbury Green–Bursledon†	Apr 1926
—	—	—	Gosport–Stubbington–Fareham	Apr 1927
36	61b	75	Fareham–Titchfield–Lee on Solent	May 1927
36	53a	54	,, – ,, –Botley	Sept 1927
—	59	80	,, – ,, –Bursledon	Nov 1928
—	—	—	Gosport–Alverstoke*	Jul 1929
—	—	—	Fareham–Segensworth–Bursledon	May 1930
—	61a	73	,, –Peel Common–Lee on Solent	Jan 1931
—	61	73a	,, –Hill Head–Lee on Solent	Feb 1932

* Relinquished in favour of other operator

† Discontinued March 1927

Route number series introduced: (a) 1927; (b) 1940; (c) 1946

BURSLEDON, NETLEY AND WOOLSTON

A few yards to the north of the Hoverterminal at Southampton —on land flattened by a landmine in 1941—stand the cruciform remains of the Crosshouse. In its prime, it sheltered travellers who wished to cross by boat to Itchen village. But in 1836, the Floating

Bridge Company had opened the chain ferry and the boatman turned to more sophisticated work. The ferry's landfall on the eastern bank was made to the south of Itchen and a new settlement grew up around it—at a place called Woolston.

By the end of the nineteenth century, the shipbuilding industry had spread along most of the river Itchen's east bank, encompassing Itchen and Woolston, both villages being part of the short-lived Itchen Rural District. During the period 1904–10, horse-drawn omnibuses were granted licences by this authority, but the records are by no means complete. There seems little doubt that Thomas Samuel Phipps was the first to trade with motor vehicles in 1912. By November 1915, Phipps had founded the Netley Motor Works Ltd, with a fleet of small 5–8 seaters, offering places to the general public as well as the increasing number of walking-wounded from the Royal Victoria Military Hospital at Netley.

Petrol restrictions dictated a return to horse traffic, however, and until the end of 1918, the only public service licences granted for motor traffic went to A. V. Roe Ltd, the aircraft manufacturers of Hamble.

In 1920, Southampton moved its boundary eastward and Itchen Rural District Council ceased to function. It had survived just long enough to issue the first licences to the Woolston, Bursledon & District Motor Service Ltd—a consortium formed by Messrs Sinclair, Burrows, Turner and Eldridge and based upon the latter's Manor House Hotel at Old Netley. A garage had been built opposite in the spring of 1919 and a service between the Cliff Hotel, Woolston and the Swan at Bursledon commenced, to be extended to Sarisbury Green and Warsash. Today's concrete bridge at Bursledon was still a planners dream: in its place stood the narrow and notorious Bursledon Toll Bridge. Whilst the driver paid the toll from his bag, the unfortunate passengers—whatever the weather—were required to walk across and rejoin the bus on the other side—in order that the combined weight did not exceed the imposed limit. Connections were provided at Lower Swanwick (on the east bank of the bridge) by Provincial for Gosport and Fuger for Fareham.

Hants & Dorset's acquisition of this Provincial route had brought the company within 4 miles of Woolston. Although the forthcoming purchase was in line with company policy, it was to be as a result of expansion from Gosport, rather than a direct step across the river from Southampton. The goodwill of the Woolston, Bursledon and Warsash service was acquired in April 1926, together with the leasehold of the garage at Old Netley, which became the 'Bursledon Depot'. Because the two Daimler 'Charabuses' installed there were considerably heavier than those previously operated through to Warsash, they worked the section from the Cliff Hotel to the toll bridge, whilst Gosport-based 'Charabuses' rendezvoused on the other side. If there were parcels to exchange, the conductors marched steadfastly to the centre.

Across the road from Woolston's Cliff Hotel forecourt—in Hazel Road—stood the modernised fleet of Thomas Phipps. Painted dark blue and operating under the name 'Royal Victoria', his vehicles now ran beyond Netley to Butlocks Hill and Hamble, with half-hourly departures on weekdays and a reduced timetable on Sundays. Buses, goodwill and garage were purchased outright on 1 November 1926—the Vulcans and Berliets of Royal Victoria acquiring Hants & Dorset livery. The Bursledon depot was closed forthwith, the buses being transferred to the premises in New Road, Netley.

Two 'Charabuses' and four ex-Phipps vehicles formed the original stable at Netley and Inspector Harry Barnes was 'posted' from Bournemouth to take up the management. He was installed in a little wooden office beside the market hall—'over the wall' as the crews called it. An early facility offered the travelling public was a book of one dozen Residents Tickets (a similar facility was available between Sandbanks and County Gates in Dorset), but this was withdrawn within the year. Soon after, the roof of the garage was jacked up to take double deckers. The Leyland 'GH7' open topper was the main type shedded there until 1933; three giant Leyland 'Leviathans' joining them in 1929. On these, the brass bell-head at the top of the stairs was so stiff that several conductors carried a whistle as an alternative method of signalling the driver. 'Blowing your whistle was a darned sight less painful than thumping that thing', said one.

From the early twenties, the name 'Supermarine' became synonymous with that of Woolston. Starting as Pemberton-Billing's during World War I, the company's first peace-time venture was a seaplane service to the Channel Islands (Woolston was one of the world's first airports). Then a large proportion of the works' effort went into the production of high-speed craft, the Schneider Trophy seaplanes. This meant extra business for Hants & Dorset for, besides the growing number of workers, scores of extra

SUMMARY OF ROUTE COMMENCEMENT DATES

(a)	(b)	(c)		
23	59	80	Woolston–Manor X Roads–Bursledon	Apr 1926
22	56	81	„ –Netley–Hamble	Nov 1926
—	—	—	„ –Bitterne–West End–Hedge End	Dec 1926
—	—	—	„ –Netley–Butlocks–Newtown–Woolston (circular)	Aug 1930
—	56a	81a	„ –Manor X Roads–Hamble	Sept 1930
—	59	80	„ –Bursledon–Fareham	Jul 1935
—	64	78	„ – „ –Warsash	„ „
—	58	79	„ – „ –Gosport	Apr 1936

Route number series introduced: (a) 1927; (b) 1940; (c) 1946

passengers were carried to the Floating Bridge, where a grandstand view could be had of the latest craft on the slipway or moored in the river. Even if it was a poor day for flying there was always a good chance of watching one of the director's hydroplanes. Whilst a stone's throw to the south, the staccato roar of the riveter's mallets echoed across the water from Thornycroft's yard and periodically, a graceful new hull slipped into the Itchen amid a chorus of toots from the waiting tugs and the more bass notes of the liners on the quays opposite. Shipwrights, riveters, planemakers and sightseers, they all came to Woolston—and Hants & Dorset brought them by the bus load. Throughout this exciting period of aero-marine history, Hants & Dorset's double deckers lined up beside the Supermarine works in Hazel Road. But it was many years later that this proximity became a distinct hazard—and it was not until the factory lay in ruins that the company moved its base from Netley to Woolston.

WINCHESTER AND EASTLEIGH

Winchester, the ancient capital of the Anglo-Saxon kings, clearly qualifies as one of our 'earlier' centres of passenger transport and, as late as the nineteenth century, its position astride the Southampton–London and Bristol–Portsmouth roads guaranteed a regular flow of 'through traffic'. But, as elsewhere, the coming of the London & South Western Railway—and, later, the Great Western—spelled the demise of the stage coach, and road passenger transport became the prerogative of the carrier's waggon.

A local syndicate first mooted a series of motor wagonette routes in April 1905. From the city centre, services to Alresford and Petersfield, Kings Worthy, Twyford—and a shorter one to St Cross—were planned, but do not seem to have materialised. W. Jones of Hursley introduced his carrier service to Winchester as late as 1906, but this still relied upon the horse. Jones did not become motorised until 1912, but nevertheless, he was probably one of the fathers of the Winchester motor bus, for Chisnell's 'King Alfred' services commenced as military transport some three years later.

As mentioned in Chapter Five, a Bournemouth & District Leyland (probably No 24, EL 4543) was sent to the city in February 1920, but the decision to rename the company—although not officially implemented until July—had already been taken by that date and, as the services proper got under way, the vehicles acquired the 'Hants & Dorset' title. One bus was outstationed at the George Yard, but as traffic increased, this arrangement became inadequate. In 1922, Redman's Garage Ltd let their Station Hill premises to the company, who later secured from the same source a contract for the purchase of land and three cottages. A parcels office and waiting room were opened in the Broadway and Inspector E. G. Tilley—another of the company's original drivers—arrived from Bournemouth to supervise. With the establishment of a second route to Southampton, running via Twyford and Swaythling and later providing connections with the Petersfield service at Fair Oak, Hants & Dorset arrived at Eastleigh. A series of routes from Eastleigh Station forecourt to the surrounding villages followed and became an additional responsibility for George Tilley. Answering a call for a more direct route to Petersfield, the company also introduced a service which began at the Broadway waiting room and ran via Cheriton, Bramdean and West Meon.

Throughout the middle twenties, the company's timetables announced that connections for Andover and Ludgershall could be made at Winchester with buses provided by 'Messrs. Mobility Ltd'. The proprietors, Anna Valley Motors of Andover, sold this undertaking to Hants & Dorset on 18 June 1927, for a reputed £3,000—£1,000 for the goodwill of the service and £1,000 apiece for the two remaining Dennis buses (HR 2646–7). These continued to operate in their original yellow livery for several months, until replaced by Leyland 'Lions'—two of which were outstationed for a while at Anna Valley to the south of Andover. Hants & Dorset split the journey into two sections: Winchester–Andover became service No 38 and, in the brief period before it was relinquished in favour of Wilts & Dorset Motor Services Ltd, the Andover–Weyhill–Appleshaw and Ludgershall route became No 39. The agreement with Wilts & Dorset led to outstation facilities being provided for one vehicle at the new garage which that company built in Junction Road, Andover.

At the southern end of the route, an office and garage for nine buses was built in Stockbridge Road, Winchester and opened in that same year. Two years later it was already too small and the number of staff employed at Winchester had risen to thirty. Some of the extra traffic came as a result of the purchase of George Trott's 'Grey Line Service', which had started running between West Meon and Winchester in 1921.

Tom Brackston was one of six crew members outstationed at Andover. Among the vehicles allocated to the section were the Lancia saloons and Leyland 'Lion' once owned by Cousin of

Lyndhurst fame, still fitted with its light alloy engine and tuned to run at 50mph. This he remembers as the most sought-after bus at Winchester—not so much for its speed, but its light clutch and sensitive response to the controls. Uppermost in his memory, however, is the dislike shown by the majority of the Winchester-based crews for the Andover run during the lean end of the season. The culprit was a low-lying mist, which turned to thick fog with little warning:

> Once the fog came down when we were due to make the last run back to Andover. Mr. Tilley came out and asked if we could get home, because there was a full load who wished to make the journey. We agreed and set out, but it got so bad that my conductor had to get out and start walking with a newspaper on his back so that I could see where to steer. It wasn't until we'd gone a good half mile beyond Three Maids Hill, that we discovered we'd taken the Crawley road instead of the Sutton Scotney—and had to back up even more slowly and try again. It took over four hours to complete that trip, during which time my conductor, the poor chap, had walked all the way from Winchester to the Town Hall, Andover.

Plans for a bus station in the city were laid during the early thirties. This was constructed on the north side of the main thoroughfare—the Broadway—and opened on Thursday, 20 June 1935. Councillor J. O. Hodder, the Lord Mayor of Winchester, cut the ribbon stretched across the entrance with a pair of golden scissors, upon which was a painting in enamel depicting a company omnibus. It was not the best of days for an official opening—the rain poured continually and the first arrival from Southampton, a Leyland 'Titan' (AD 172), was delayed by a traffic jam caused when a large ship's propeller was taken through the narrow streets. An interesting bonus, however, was the Roman remains discovered during the construction work and which were later placed on display in the passengers' waiting room.

Apart from the introduction of route variations on the Andover service, there was little room for further pre-war expansion in the area. Throughout the thirties, the other operators—Aldershot & District, Winchester & District, Venture Ltd, Greyfriars and—in particular—Chisnell's 'King Alfred' retained a firm hold upon their licences. Meanwhile, the company's close managerial relationship with Aldershot & District meant that a system of 'through tickets' between Southampton and Aldershot, Alton and Alresford could be introduced.

Only two other operators' licences were acquired in the middle thirties—Richard Miller, operating under the name 'Santoy' (the horse which won him enough money to buy his first charabanc), relinquished his Fair Oak to Eastleigh service in June 1934 and Percy Lambert—'The Little Wonder Bus Service'—his East Meon, Langrish and Petersfield route in September 1936.

SUMMARY OF ROUTE COMMENCEMENT DATES

(a)	(b)	(c)		
20	47	47	Winchester–Chandlers Ford–Southampton	Feb 1920
21	48	49	" –Eastleigh–Fair Oak– "	Nov 1920
40	45	66	" –Hursley–Romsey– " (1)	Nov 1921
25	54	69	" –Bishops Waltham–Fareham	Dec 1922
—	—	—	" –Fareham–Portsmouth (2)	Apr 1923
27	41	41	Eastleigh–Allbrook–Brambridge	Apr 1924
30	46	46	" –Chandlers Ford–Hursley	" "
31	42	42a	" –Bishopstoke–Stoke Common	" "
25	54	69	Winchester–Fareham–Gosport	Jul 1924
18	49	67	" –Cheriton–Petersfield	May 1925
—	—	44	Eastleigh–West End–Botley	Sept 1925
38	55	68	Winchester–Sutton Scotney–Andover	June 1927
39	—	—	Andover–Weyhill–Ludgershall (3)	" "
40	45	66	Winchester–Hursley–Romsey	Sept 1927
40	45	—	" – " – " –Lyndhurst	May 1928
—	44	44	Eastleigh–Horton Heath (Hants)	Jul 1928
—	43	43a	Fair Oak–Lower Upham–Bishops Waltham	" "
—	—	45	Eastleigh–Otterbourne	Jan 1929
—	55a	68a	Winchester–Barton Stacey–Andover	Sept 1932
—	55b	68b	" –Crawley Down– "	Jun 1940

(1) Discontinued March 1922
(2) Curtailed at Fareham Feb 1926
(3) Relinquished in favour of Wilts & Dorset

Route number series introduced: (a) 1927; (b) 1940; (c) 1946

CHAPTER SEVEN

THE TOURS DEPARTMENT 1935–1945

ROYAL BLUE

ANDERSON & FRANKIS have described* how the long-established firm of Elliott Brothers (Royal Blue) was acquired by the Tilling organisation in February 1935, thus releasing Hants & Dorset from their pledge of 1924 and placing at their disposal a fleet of 38 touring coaches.

To facilitate the company's re-entry into the tours and excursion business, many of the Royal Blue staff remained at Bournemouth: H. W. Rollings, appointed tours manager, had served as general manager for Royal Blue since 1921. Now, as the fleet was split three ways between Southern and Western National and Hants & Dorset, he was able to choose the vehicles which were to remain at Bournemouth. Major buildings acquired were the Holdenhurst Road Garage and the Pavilion Garage near Bournemouth Pier. The former, the original Royal Blue Express Coach Station, was later acquired by Shamrock & Rambler Coaches, but the Pavilion premises were retained. These had been built on a speculative basis by a local contractor and comprised a large garage, offices—and a restaurant known as the Corner House Cafe: the Daimler limousines of Elliott Brothers' private hire fleet had been based there. Hants & Dorset now turned it into a base for their newly acquired fleet of coaches and sent the cars across to the St Michael's Road garage.

* *History of Royal Blue Express Services*, David & Charles, 1970.

The Isle of Wight circular tour was an interesting aspect of the new work. Elliott Brothers had devised an excursion which left Bournemouth for Lymington, where the coaches were transported across the Solent in barges. Members of the Bolton Cooperative Society had paid 2 guineas (£2.10) per head to become the first fare-paying passengers. Surprisingly, this was 12s (60p) more than it would have cost them in 1970! In 1922, a garage was built at Yarmouth, IoW, utilising parts left over from the extension of the Rutland Road premises in Bournemouth. Erected in

ROYAL BLUE COACHES. PRIVATE HIRE CAR DEPARTMENT.

A HIRE SERVICE OF QUALITY

The very Latest Daimler Cars for every need. Social Calls. Theatres. Dances. Shopping. Stations

A few examples from our Private Hire Car Tariff.

	*Pavilion & Th'tre	Central Station	West Station	Boscombe	Winton	Moordown
WEST CLIFF	5/–	2/6	2/–	3/6	3/6	4/6
EAST CLIFF	5/–	2/–	3/–	2/–	3/6	4/–
WESTBOURNE	6/6	3/6	2/6	5/–	4/–	5/–
MEYRICK OR TALBOT PARKS	5/–	2/6	2/6	3/6	2/–	3/–
BOSCOMBE	6/–	2/6	3/6	—	3/6	4/6
DEAN OR RICHMOND PARKS AND SPRINGBOURNE	5/–	2/6	3/6	2/6	3/–	3/6
LOWER CHARMINSTER, KING'S OR QUEEN'S PARK...	6/6	3/–	3/6	3/–	3/–	3/–
MOORDOWN	7/6	4/–	4/6	4/6	3/–	—
WINTON	6/–	3/–	3/6	3/6	—	3/–
FISHERMAN'S WALK	7/6	4/6	5/6	3/–	7/6	7/6

* Fares from Theatres are inclusive of Outward and Return Journeys.

OUTINGS.—All Classes of Firms, Clubs and Associations catered for. Special Quotations with detailed Itineraries, submitted immediately upon application. Let us quote you! Satisfaction Guaranteed. Only the very Latest Type of Coaches provided.

'Phone: Bournemouth 6333.

Hants & Dorset (Royal Blue) private hire car tariff: March 1935

Mill Road, it could house 6 coaches and removed the costly business of shipping them across the water. By the end of 1921, this Royal Blue tour had killed off a rival enterprise operated jointly by Hants & Dorset and the violet charabancs of the Yarmouth (IW) Touring Company Ltd. Service buses from Bournemouth and Southampton had been met at Lymington by one of the Yarmouth company's launches.

Hants & Dorset took over the garage and contents (one Leyland 'Tiger' and 5 AEC 'Regals' with Duple 'crash-proof' bodywork) in time for the 1935 season and placed a company driver, Percy Mussell, in charge upon the island. The intinerary, made in a clockwise direction from Yarmouth, remained unchanged: Shalfleet–Carisbrooke–Newport–Whippingham–East Cowes–Binstead–Ryde (lunch)–Brading–Sandown–Shanklin (halt)–Ventnor–Undercliff Drive–Niton–Blackgang (halt)–Military Road–Freshwater Bay–Farringford–Alum Bay (tea)–Colwell, returning to Yarmouth in time for the 6.25 ferry to Lymington. Two drivers were based upon the island and four others came over with each party from the mainland. When demand proved heavy, extra coaches and drivers were hired from the Fountain Garage at Cowes.

NEW COACHES

Initially, it was decided to retain the familiar Royal Blue colour and fleetname upon the company's new coaches. Fourteen had arrived by May 1935, fitted with attractive semi-observation bodywork incorporating many features designed by Brush Electrical Engineering Company draughtsman, Albert Quenby. In the event, Brush built only one example, which they exhibited upon their stand at the 1935 Commercial Motor Show—and delivered to Hants & Dorset the following March. By 1939, thirty-seven Leyland chassis had been fitted with bodies in the same style, built by John C. Beadle Ltd of Dartford, Kent. Seventeen elderly chassis were similarly rebodied. But for the war, others would have followed. If anything, the exterior shape of the Dartford product proved a shade easier on the eye, because of a more graceful termination of structural line, but a peak of aesthetic perfection was reached after the 1936 season, when a cleverly proportioned green and cream livery replaced the original. In this form, they rank among the most elegant motor coaches ever operated. However, several writers have suggested that the design was a Hants & Dorset exclusive. It must be said that this is not so, for Hill's Coaches of West Bromwich were offering seven-day tours in 1935 with structurally identical vehicles.

Page 139 (*left*) B. H. Ransom, founder of Tourist; (*right*) Pooling his resources with those of S. C. Bullock, Tourist Motor Coaches (Southampton) Ltd was formed. This Leyland Cub displays the once familiar trade-mark designed by Robert Morse

Hants & Dorset placed this Wadham-bodied Thornycroft 'Lightning' coach in service in 1935. For one season, it was painted dark blue and turquoise—and marked Tourist, Southampton

Page 140 (*above*) If one wished to catch a train, a telephone call to the Lymington depot would bring Driver 'Budgell' Stride and his Leyland Cub to the door; (*below*) this 1939 Cub coach was refitted as a bus in 1950, a policy since adopted for all Hants & Dorset's elderly coaches

TOURIST MOTOR COACHES (SOUTHAMPTON) LTD

For a few months, the Southampton agency for Royal Blue Express Services remained with Elliott Brothers' agents, Holland Coaches of Grosvenor Square. Meanwhile, the negotiations for the transfer to the company of Tourist Motor Coaches (Southampton) Ltd, Tours & Excursion Department had reached an advanced stage.

Bertie H. Ransom bought his first two charabancs—American GMCs—in 1919, garaging them in Southampton's one-time famous old Back-of-the-Walls. He also had garages in Leighton and St Mary's Roads and in the period up to 1927 added a dozen more vehicles to his fleet. Ransom's regular runs to London started when, as a direct result of the General Strike in 1926, he met the *Mauretania* and other large liners at the docks with 26-seat Karrier charabancs and provided the passengers with a means of reaching the capital.

On 7 November 1927, Ransom pooled his resources with those of S. C. Bullock from Lancashire and Tourist Motor Coaches (Southampton) Ltd, was formed. Bullock had previously been managing director of Pendle Road Services of Blackburn. Ribble had purchased the goodwill of this company and secured from the general manager and his partner, Thomas Briggs, an undertaking that they would not set up another omnibus company within one hundred miles of Ribble territory. Accordingly, they came to Southampton, and after discussions with Ransom, decided that the establishment of the London Express Service was a much more viable proposition than setting up stage carriage services in opposition to Hants & Dorset. With them they brought Lee Fletcher, a traffic schedule expert, two inspectors and four drivers, who—with Ransom's drivers and maintenance staff—completed the personnel of the new company. Simultaneously, W. A. Browne's Hiawatha Motor Coaches (previously Hiawatha & Queen) was purchased, together with premises in Winchester Road, which at the time still bore the name of the

NEDERLAND LINE ROYAL DUTCH MAIL

IN SAMENWERKING MET

TOURIST

MOTOR COACHES

1 GROSVENOR SQUARE, SOUTHAMPTON. PHONE 4001

EXCURSIE No. 3 - DONDERDAG.

Naar Milford-on-Sea

Vertrek van het schip 2 u.n.m.

DEZE toer wordt gemaakt via Totton en "the New Forest" naar Lyndhurst. Men wyst U het z.g. "Queen's House," een bouwwerk uit den tyd van Charles II. George III hield zich hier een week op tydens zyn reis naar Weymouth in 1789.

Na vertrek van Lyndhurst langs een anderen weg door het Bosch, wordt te Knightwood gestopt ter bezichtiging van de Knightwood-Eik, een boom, die de grootste van Groot Brittannie wordt genoemd.

Te Milford-on-Sea wordt in het Cliff Café de thee gebruikt. Men heeft hier een prachtig gezicht op het eiland Wight.

De terugweg gaat via de oude dorpjes en stadjes Pennington, Lymington, Brockenhurst en Lyndhurst naar het schip, alwaar men tegen 6 u.n.m. arriveert.

Prys (inclusief thee) **11s. 0d.**

'UITSTAPJES IN SOUTHAMPTON' One of the many foreign-language brochures—this one in Dutch—produced by Tourist in the early thirties

business previously operated by Browne's father, The Vivid Touring Company. A new garage was built on this site, measuring 300ft × 125ft and incorporating five inspection pits, machine shop, coach painting and trimming departments. When the re-shaped service commenced a fitter was available there 24 hours a day.

The registered office was then moved from St Mary's Road to Grosvenor Square (see p 74, *The History of Royal Blue Express Services*, which also includes a record of Tourist express services). Over the seven and a half years of its existence, the company possessed a total of some fifty coaches. The range of local and long-distance tours offered was the largest in Southampton. In 1933, eight further vehicles were added to the fleet, following the purchase of Jackson's Low Level Safety Coaches—otherwise known as Coliseum Coaches—based upon the Savoy Hotel: the coach proprietor, J. Jackson, became Tours Manager for his new employers.

Thomas Tilling Ltd, began negotiations for the purchase of Tourist in November 1934, as a direct result of an initiative by William Graham, who urged the proprietors that the approaches of several interested parties should be set aside until his directors had been consulted. Thus, the Tours and Excursion Department was taken over complete by Hants & Dorset in May 1935. This included the staff—J. Jackson retaining his post—the Grosvenor Square station, the garage in Winchester Road, ten Leyland 'Tiger' coaches and—at Jackson's request—a small capacity Albion from the Coliseum fleet. Twenty-four other vehicles went to Southern and Western National at Exeter.

A tours office was then constructed at the Bedford Place entrance to the Grosvenor Square Garage and the Tourist booking-office at the Bargate closed. As with Royal Blue at Bournemouth, the familiar Tourist colours were retained until the end of the 1936 season, when a programme of re-bodying and re-painting was put in hand.

HOLLAND COACHES, ETC

The Tours Manager at Southampton then set about consolidating the Grosvenor Square headquarters. Across the square stood Capt Reginald Keevil's Southern Coastal Coaching Station —still official agents for Royal Blue Express Services—and his tours business, Holland Coaches. Keevil's station derived much of its revenue from a restaurant used by express coach passengers, but as Associated Motorways coaches began using the ex-Tourist station, custom fell rapidly. Briefly, Keevil turned the upper floor into a gymnasium, with the lower section open for independent operators and his own excursion business, but opposition across the square proved too stiff, and eventually he sold his premises, marshalling area and goodwill to Hants & Dorset on 17 September 1935. The straw yellow Holland Coaches fleet of 2 Lancias, 2 Cottin Desgoutes and 2 Willis Overland Crossleys, were taken to Winchester Road for inspection, but were found to be altogether too exotic for retention and were sold off independently.

Independent express operators were thus deprived of their Southampton agent—and Shamrock & Rambler were persuaded to open an office in the town to preserve their interest in the London–Southampton–Bournemouth express route and set up their own tours business.

Capt Keevil withdrew into the hotel business and took to the sea, operating pleasure boats from the Royal Pier. Both ventures were attended with misfortune: the pride of his fleet, the beautiful *Miss Valerie II*, sank during a spring gale in 1937 and three years later incendiary bombs wrecked his hotel.

On the same day as the Holland Coaches purchase, the company acquired Beamish & Hapgood's Rob Roy Coaches of Arthur Road and Anglesey Road, Shirley. F. H. Beamish was a real veteran, having started at Bournemouth in 1911 with a horse charabanc. In partnership with A. E. Hapgood, the work had been of a seasonal nature, with the coaches stored during the winter.

Meanwhile, at Bournemouth, new Tours Manager H. W. Rollings had not been idle. In a three-year period, the following businesses were acquired:

March 1935: C. W. Wallis. White Heather Motor Coaches. Garage in Exeter Road. Two Thornycroft coaches operated in white and green livery. Goodwill only acquired.

August 1935: E. R. & E. M. Whitren. Billies Coaches. Following the acquisition by the company of their stage-carriage services, the Whitrens operated a GMC and a Bedford 'WLB' upon tours work from a garage at Pennington, near Lymington. The latter vehicle and the goodwill of the business were acquired.

September 1935: Mrs G. Price & Jack W. Roddy.

Registered as Byways Ltd, their fleet of 2 Thornycrofts and a Lancia had operated from Sea Road, Boscombe. The vehicles, which were cream with one red band, were not purchased.

September 1935: Parma Violet Coaches.

Operated by Messrs Logan & W. A. Courtier, also from a base in Sea Road, Boscombe, the fleet consisted of 4 Thornycrofts, a Reo and a Star, all painted pale violet. One Thornycroft and the goodwill were acquired.

May 1936: W. H. Mondon & A. J. Sedwell.

Tours and excursion business operated from Exeter Road—reputedly under the revived name, White Heather. Goodwill only.

February 1937: J. A. Bright & R. W. Gardner.

Trading as Gem Coach Tours from Holdenhurst Road, this partnership also held a licence to operate a fantail tour in Scotland. The fleet consisted of three turquoise Lancias, which were not taken. Bournemouth Corporation granted permission for the company to use the stand for coaches in Durley Road, previously used by Gem Coaches.

August 1938: Symes & Son. Enterprise Motor Coaches.

Based in Tregonwell Road, with a booking office at Malmesbury and Parsons's Dairy in The Square, a trio of cream coaches were operated—a McCurd, a Dodge and a Bedford 'WTB'. Goodwill only acquired.

SEEING BRITAIN TOURS

Afternoon, evening and full day excursions were now operated from Bournemouth, Poole, Lymington, Southampton and other points near these towns. Agents with booking facilities were established, each exhibiting a board marked HANTS & DORSET, ROYAL BLUE AND TOURIST. Departing from Bournemouth and Southampton, three- to sixteen-day Seeing Britain Tours were introduced, running as far afield as Wales and Scotland and were an integrated series based upon the various tours recently acquired. By 1939, the company were operating a fleet of sixty-three coaches and hiring many more. The original 'Royal Blue' Daimler hire-car fleet was replaced with unmarked Humber Snipe limousines, which could again be hired together with a uniformed chauffeur.

The coaches quickly paid for themselves. In March 1935, before the commencement of coach operation, the company had declared a net profit of £53,318: two years later the figure was £63,720—after deductions for further acquisitions, extensions to

November 1935: Humber hire cars replace the Daimlers

Bournemouth bus station and the purchase of the freehold of the Royal Mews. Stage carriage profits were also on the increase and a new era of confidence and expansion was threatened only by the growing clouds of war. In October 1937, 50,000 £1 shares were distributed to existing shareholders in the proportion of one for every eight held and an increase in capital was authorised from the existing £550,000 to £700,000—at which figure it was to stand for the next sixteen years. (For further details, see Appendix B.)

WORLD WAR II

Upon the declaration of war, all tours and excursion work was suspended. Fourteen Leyland Tiger coaches were requisitioned by the War Department in 1940—at the time of the Dunkirk evacuation. Therefore a pleasant little story which once circulated the Engineering Department is probably apocryphal, but worth the telling: it appears that when the Allied forces were sweeping across Normandy in 1944, an army engineer trained at Shirley Road came across a Beadle-bodied coach, which he took to be a Hants & Dorset, painted in Wehrmacht grey with appropriate Teutonic insignia and numbering. No doubt, if the Germans had found one abandoned at Dunkirk, they would have appreciated its luxurious appointment—and certainly used it, but if both the official records and this story are to be believed, it just might have been one from Hills of West Bromwich. What can be stated with certainty is that the remaining company coaches joined the invasion stand-by fleet. That no German soldiers reached our shores perhaps saved the company some embarrassment. There would have been the vague possibility that 32 of them came part of the way by Hants & Dorset.

CHAPTER EIGHT

WORLD WAR II AND PEACE

EMERGENCY REGULATIONS

ON SATURDAY, 22 May 1937, a 'long line' of Hants & Dorset buses was sent to Southampton Docks to meet the *Habana* carrying Basque children, refugees from the Spanish Civil War. They were taken first to the baths on the Western Esplanade and then to a specially-built camp at North Stoneham. The mixed emotions witnessed then, proved a foretaste of what was yet in store. Later, many were found temporary homes in private houses throughout Southampton and district. Within months, those housed in the eastern part of the borough were living cheek by jowl with large numbers of aircraft engineers, drafted in to work on the Supermarine factory's most magnificent product—the Spitfire. Compulsorily billeted upon those householders who had room to spare, they were conveyed in their hundreds to the factory at Woolston by Netley-based buses.

Throughout 1939, personnel enlisted in the air raid precautions units as they were formed and took turns to handle the fire-fighting equipment. Large supplies of sandbags, fire buckets and gummed paper for the windows of company offices were delivered in the hard-pressed vehicles of the service fleet. In the last week of August, the first barrage balloons went up over Southampton. Within days, bus services were delayed when the Woolston Police Station balloon lost its gas and trailed a quarter of a mile of cable across rooftops and roadways in a series of sad loops. Southampton's schoolchildren were already being evacuated—district by district—ushered aboard the buses and trains by Southampton footballers, acting in their new role as special policemen. The crews parked beside the Supermarine factory in Woolston began to take a new interest in the Queen Mary trailers,* now moving off and up the Portsmouth Road at regular intervals.

Regulations concerning the lighting of vehicles now came into force. Maintenance crews set about the brackets holding the headlamps and bent them downwards to reduce the beam—a task performed too well, for the drivers couldn't see beyond the pool of light. Instead, the near-side bulb was removed and the off-side lamp masked, an arrangement which proved fairly satisfactory until slotted hoods were fitted to both headlamps. To identify the danger points dumb irons were painted white and white lines traced around the mudguards and wheel arches. Various schemes were tried with interior lighting: an early experiment with blue lacquer proved so depressing for day-time travellers that it was quickly dropped—it had been painted over the windows and gave a good impression of travel in a hearse. It was realised that a much easier plan would be to remove some of the light bulbs and dip the remainder in the lacquer. At Bournemouth's Royal Mews, trials were carried out with a mini-torch suspended from a rail along the roof of the saloon and powered from the vehicle's battery, but this did not become general practice and conductors and inspectors worked through the gloom with small torches attached to their shoulder straps.

Following the declaration of war on Sunday, 3 September 1939, much of this effort seemed wasted as bus services throughout southern Hampshire ceased working one hour after sunset. The very last were the 9.15pm, arrivals at Lymington and Bishops Waltham; the final journeys to Fareham, Bournemouth and Southampton arriving at 9pm, precisely. In Dorset, later journeys were run as usual—and gradually these were restored farther east as the first nervous weeks of the war passed without incident. In October the country was divided into Emergency Transport Regions: Gosport and Fareham based buses worked from within Area 6B (which included Portsmouth and the Isle of Wight),

* Extra-long aircraft-transporters, named after the *RMS Queen Mary* when it was the world's longest ship.

whilst those at Southampton, Winchester, Bournemouth and Poole were in Area 6C. This meant that in an emergency, District Transport Officers, at Portsmouth and Southampton respectively, could present contingency plans before the depots at very short notice: an arrangement which was to be put into effect the following May.

DUNKIRK AND ITS AFTERMATH

On Saturday, 11 May 1940, passengers and conductors swapped tales of the previous night's excitement. For the first time searchlights had swept the sky and guns between Gosport and Southampton had fired at an enemy reconnaissance aircraft. Although the sirens had not sounded, this was warning enough and a policy of vehicle dispersal was introduced. Thereafter drivers were encouraged to take their buses home each evening and leave them in the street, following their immobilisation by the removal of the rotor-arm.

Within days, the little paddle-steamer *Gracie Fields*—now simply 'J 100', in a coat of naval grey—slipped her moorings above the Floating Bridge on a one-way trip to Dunkirk. On her way down Southampton Water, she passed the first of the many vessels of all shapes and sizes which brought French civilians and soldiers seeking refuge in England. The DTO alerted the company's Southampton depot and Hants & Dorset buses went in convoy to the docks to deal with the traffic. It required every available vehicle which could be spared and drivers, inspectors and regulators worked far beyond their normal hours operating a seemingly endless shuttle service. After resting several days in local schools, many of the French troops were returned to the docks, from whence they sailed for the western coast of France in a futile attempt to stem the enemy advance. A second withdrawal kept the company's vehicles busy well into the third week in June.

The British Expeditionary Force had lost all its transport on the beaches of Dunkirk. An 'Emergency Powers (Defence) Acquisition and Disposal of Motor Vehicles Order, 1940' came into immediate effect—and nineteen Hants & Dorset Leyland coaches and saloons went off to serve with the military. The threat of invasion now loomed large. Apart from delays caused whilst mines were sown beneath the roadways, road blocks and tank traps constructed, daily services were depleted by the temporary loss of further single-deck vehicles. These were placed on stand-by at Army and Naval barracks, ready to rush troops into action wherever the enemy landed.

AIR RAIDS

During the first air-raid alerts, drivers stopped their vehicles at the nearest shelter and shepherded their passengers inside—emerging only when the all-clear had sounded. Thus one reconnaissance aircraft crossing the coast at Portsmouth could paralyse bus services all the way to Southampton. There were many such interruptions until the drivers began to take upon themselves the responsibility of assessing the nature of the alert and stopping only when danger positively threatened. The main fear in the towns was the effect that bomb blast would have upon a high-sided bus, whilst in the countryside, there was the distinct possibility that the buses might be singled out for attack.

The first bombs fell upon the town of Southampton in the early hours of Thursday, 20 June. A grocer's shop in Obelisk Road, Woolston suffered a direct hit. Although this was nearly one mile from the Supermarine factory, the message was perfectly clear—to the local citizens, if not yet to the Luftwaffe. The factory was an obvious target for a concentrated attack—and Hants & Dorset buses terminating their journeys at Woolston parked under its very walls. Despite this, the Hamble buses continued to depart from their usual stand, the Fareham-bound from the Cliff Hotel forecourt opposite and the Southampton Corporation vehicles from the equally vulnerable Floating Bridge Hard. The only concession toward this 'front-line' position was the provision of a two-man metal bell shelter for the use of corporation crews. Yet, another two months were to elapse before further bombs were dropped within the borough—and not until Sunday, 15 September that the factory was singled out for a determined attack. Bus crews sought shelter in Portsmouth Road and in the basement of the Cliff Hotel. Despite a heavy barrage from the anti-aircraft guns in Grange Lane, the bombers came through unharmed—whilst their unchallenged fighter escort amused themselves by shooting up the balloons. At the all-clear the factory remained intact, bill heads from a shattered furniture store were still fluttering to earth and the cream roofs of the buses were covered in a layer of red brick dust. Only three windows were broken in an upper saloon of one double decker. Another attempt was made on 24 September, resulting in great loss of life. This raid caused a further exodus of householders to friends in the countryside, with considerably more standing-passengers than the official eight aboard the buses. Delayed action bombs had been dropped and these now hastened each departure with explosions which hurled asphalt and paving stones skywards like vicious black lightning.

The Supermarine works was finally wrecked the following Thursday afternoon, when a large attacking force carpet-bombed the area. On this occasion, the sirens had given plenty of warning; the workers ran from the factory and joined a fast mixed convoy of Hants & Dorset and corporation buses up the rise of Portsmouth Road. For brief minutes, the scene resembled a speeded-up film of supporters leaving a football match. The runners poured into the nearest shelters and the buses swung away at intervals to park under the flimsy protection of trees—some as far away as Wrights Hill. But as students of the Battle of Britain know, the dispersal of the factory was almost complete and the Spitfire continued in production at shadow factories. Eventually the site was cleared and for many years the concrete floor where Spitfires had been assembled became a parking lot for the company's buses.

Attacks against Portsmouth and Gosport had developed somewhat earlier. On Friday, 16 August, dive-bombers attacked the RAF field at Gosport and the naval one at Lee on Solent. H. A. F. Annalls recalls:

> 'After the all-clear sounded, I set off again in my "E-type" (a Leyland TD 1) and was bowling up to the top of the Rowner Railway Arch when I saw that the middle was missing. I just managed to stop in time and reversed back into a field.'

The Luftwaffe had nearly claimed a company bus, yet it was not until January of the following year that two were destroyed. These were G 120 and the almost new TS 804, lost at Gosport. With them went the garage and other premises, whilst an employee suffered severe injuries. To the north, Fareham depot survived, despite fire-bomb attacks. Writing in the *Hants & Dorset Motor Services Magazine*, D. J. Holt records that:

> . . . several incendiary bombs penetrated the roof on more than one occasion and, in one raid, a bus left the garage in a hurry with a fire-bomb actually lodged in the near side front wheel hub, looking as it went like a large Catherine Wheel, the bomb finally being dislodged as the bus turned the first right hand corner.

Meanwhile, two buses had suffered minor damage from aerial machine-gun fire. This attack hastened the completion of the task already in hand—the application of grey paint over the previously cream roofs. As the tempo of the Southampton raids increased, the policy of vehicle dispersal began to pay dividends. Drivers were now permitted to collect their neighbours each evening and drive off to the New Forest, where they parked overnight. Some operated a strict routine of 'ladies downstairs—men up, and no matter whether married or not!' Although safe from the bombs, the refugees spent many anxious moments—and none worse than the successive nights of 30 November–1 December, when bombers set the town ablaze and kept it burning for 48 hours. From as far afield as Minstead, the aircraft—picked out by searchlights—could be seen circling with apparent impunity in a tomato-red sky. Clusters of incendiaries fluttered earthwards through the glare like shoals of minnows and disappeared behind the bare branches of the trees. Disturbed by it all, Forest creatures remained awake and set up a chatter which served to make the watchers even more uneasy. At first light the buses returned, the fortunate finding their houses still standing among the now waterless fire hoses and drifting smoke. Miraculously, all the company's property remained intact. The buildings adjacent to the omnibus station in Birmingham Street had been destroyed, yet the station suffered nothing worse than the loss of a few windows and its familiar tame sparrows.

Across the park, in Grosvenor Square, fitters Reg Whitmore and Bert Atkins had been fighting fires beside the garage, when Whitmore was struck by a further incendiary. Midst fires and explosions, Atkins administered first-aid and returned to the fray —for which service he was subsequently awarded the British Empire Medal.

Leyland 'Titans' loaned to London Transport during the Blitz, returned to the south coast with this 'battle honour' fixed to the bulkhead of the lower saloon

In the weeks which followed, passes were issued to enable employees to gain access to the shattered centre of the town and these were inspected by armed troops. The company's Southampton area office promptly moved to Romsey, from whence operations were controlled until late 1944. Yet, the company's property suffered no further damage until October 1941, when a land mine blasted the rear of the Pavilion Garage in Bath Road, Bournemouth.

Many of the younger crew members were now in the armed forces and conductresses began to appear upon the platform—the first for over twenty years. Army engineer-apprentices were posted to the Shirley Road works, given a spare engine to practice upon under the eagle eye of Caleb Sutton and gained experience later put to good use in Normandy.

Devastating raids upon London had already depleted the London Transport fleet and the following Hants & Dorset buses were sent to the capital as replacements, returning with commemorative plates affixed to the bulkhead:

Leyland Titan (TD 1) E 134, 204, 206, 210, 310, 334, 338, 358.

The following also carried these plates, but are not among those listed as such in the company records:

Leyland Titan (TD 2) G 350, 356.
M 18, 34, 112, 156.

The New Year's Honours List of 1942 announced the award of the Order of the British Empire to William Wells Graham. 'This is in recognition of the many duties we have performed since the outbreak of war,' he told the employees. 'You have all earned this and I consider it an honour to accept it on your behalf.'

A TILLING COMPANY

In September 1942, Hants & Dorset's parent company, Tilling and British Automobile Traction Ltd, was wound up. Hants & Dorset Motor Services Ltd was one of the operating companies acquired by the newly formed Tilling Motor Services Ltd. An eventual Tilling monopoly had been on the cards since 1936, when a switch in management policy led to the purchase and delivery of Bristol chassis and Eastern Coachworks bodywork—both manufactured by companies under Tilling control. So ended a twenty-six year association with BET, the group which had played so large a part in the establishment of the company. Two years later, Tilling's new trade mark appeared on most Hants & Dorset literature—a drawing of Crewe House, superimposed upon a tyre which bore the words 'A Tilling Company'.

WARTIME UTILITY BUSES, ETC

The first double-decked buses built to a Ministry of War Transport specification arrived in 1942. Although four bodybuilders were involved, only minor differences were evident: all featured composite construction devoid of all embellishment, with plenty of 'sharp corners', and—in some cases—wooden slatted seats. For many passengers, these wooden seats seemed the ultimate indignity in a grey world of gas masks and food rationing. It is perhaps fortunate that the number of austerity buses did not exceed twenty.

Throughout 1943, only one bomb fell on Southampton. Yet on Sunday, 23 May, Bournemouth experienced its heaviest attack of the entire war. Bombs fell the length of Holdenhurst Road, severely damaging the Shamrock and Rambler garage, wrecking a hotel at the Lansdowne and—despite the efforts of an anti-aircraft unit on its roof—burning down Bournemouth's largest department store. Across the Bourne Stream, one high explosive bomb landed beside the omnibus station standing area. Arthur Watts recalls:

> It was just after Sunday lunchtime. When I got down there, all the windows had been blown out of the buses—not in, that was the funny thing, but out. Twenty-five buses! They had all the drivers, conductors and cleaners with hammers and bars, beating out what broken glass remained. Far too energetic, they were, and all the bent frames were sent round to Norwich Avenue in one big heap—and no idea which buses they belonged to because they were different types and sizes. I was ten days cutting glass and sorting that lot out, nothing else for ten days, with fitters and all-sorts helping. In the meantime, some of the buses went out on service without windows and with sacking at the front to keep the draught out.

Although this raid caused considerable loss of life across the town, everyone at the omnibus station had taken cover and neither passengers nor Hants & Dorset personnel suffered injury.

At about this time, the Ministry of War Transport sanctioned the conversion of existing single deckers to a peripheral seating arrangement, so that 30 seated and 30 standing passengers could be carried. This was particularly useful for the heavily patronised works services in many parts of the company area. Local papers carried regular company advertisements explaining the difficulties of war-time transport and apologising for inevitable inconveniences. One of particular note reminded passengers that fuel supplies were at a premium and declared 'Hants & Dorset are proud to announce—The Gas Producer'.

PROPULSION BY GAS

Mindful of the lessons of World War I, most Tilling companies had commenced experimental work with gas-producers in 1939. Hants & Dorset's first unit—a Gohin Poulenc—was installed in the boot of Bristol saloon TS 701, during May of that year. Another arrived in September and was fitted beneath the stairs of Leyland Titan A 528. In each case, the fuel tanks were removed and replaced with gas filtration units filled with water. In this guise, neither vehicle was completely successful. Both were affected by cylinder wear and an inexplicable susceptibility to changes in the weather. Drivers of A 528, on the Southampton–Lymington run, found that switching off the engine could only be risked in the vicinity of an experienced engineer, who could coax it back to life.

Eventually, however, a fully-operative unit for use by the Tilling companies was evolved. Insulation, furring, cylinder-wear and a host of other problems were ironed-out by W. J. Morison, Chief Engineer of the Eastern National Omnibus Company (and father of Hants & Dorset managing director, Douglas Morison). Following contributions from Bristol Tramways & Carriage Company engineers, a standard trailer unit was mass-produced. It was two-wheeled and fired with anthracite.

Fifteen double deckers and three single deckers were converted to tow these trailers, which were mainly active throughout 1943 and 1944. One powered the Fareham depot's all-grey Leyland Titan (known to the crews as 'The Old Grey Mare'). By the summer of 1944, the Mare was beginning to find the hills a little difficult and a picture of the unit remains fixed in the memory: the bus is at a standstill on Hoad's Hill. Whilst the driver looks on anxiously, a Gibraltarian conductress, her dark eyes flashing, prods at the anthracite with a long poker, giving a fair imitation of a picador and muttering Spanish epithets which, fortunately, we do not understand. Suitably charmed, The Old Grey Mare (E 332) finds some more compression and moves off.

D-DAY AND AFTER

The massive build-up of military transport to the east of Southampton, eventually brought gas-producer operations to a standstill. On hilly sections they tended to hold up, rather than help, the war effort. Their contribution made, they were gradually withdrawn.

Tanks, half-tracks, armoured cars, lorries and the largest collection of warlike paraphernalia ever assembled now stood nose-to-tail along almost every road. In Fareham it was difficult to find a paving stone unbroken by tracked vehicles. Inevitably, one-way traffic systems were introduced and bus services re-routed. Service buses leaving Fareham bus station now gingerly awaited gaps in the seemingly endless convoys of tanks which slithered into Portland Street over a specially laid concrete pad and roared off towards the embarkation points. The buses began to slither too, as large lumps of black waterproofing-compound were picked up by the tyres. There was but one solution: pick it out piece-by-piece with a screw driver!

After D-Day there was one more hardship to be endured—and it affected the eastern area only. Air-launched flying bombs, aimed at Southampton, got no farther than the eastern outskirts, but tested the nerves of everyone in the Fareham area. The depot reintroduced vehicle dispersal, but although several missiles flew directly over the garage, the company again escaped loss. The few which arrived in daylight caused the crews far less worry than conventional aircraft, for the old fear of machine-gun fire no longer existed. After the last had fallen in July 1944, the drivers could again concentrate solely upon the road ahead.

The Luftwaffe's withdrawal of manned aircraft led to a gradual restoration of peace-time liveries and de-restricted lighting. By January 1945, a large proportion of the fleet had been repainted with cream roofs in pre-war style. The company's war effort was virtually over: it was an effort of which the personnel could feel proud. With the addition of a mere twenty utility vehicles, they had maintained in remarkably fine order a fleet which succeeded in equalling the best pre-war records. Thanks to the discretion of the crews, not one passenger had been injured as a result of enemy action during the entire course of the war.

One further recognition was announced in the New Year's Honours List of 1946. H. N. Crabb, who had been appointed manager of the Southampton depot upon the retirement of W. H. Willoughby in 1942, was awarded the British Empire Medal.

WILLIAM GRAHAM'S RETIREMENT

June 1945 saw the end of an era. Although he remained a director, William Graham retired from his post of General Manager, to be succeeded by Secretary and Traffic Manager, Albert E. Webster. The General Manager of Wilts & Dorset Motor Services Ltd, Raymond Longman—already a director of Hants & Dorset—became Managing Director.

At the retirement party which followed, the depot managers presented the Founder with a set of suitably inscribed gold cuff links and dress studs. On the behalf of the employees, the perennial William Cox gave him a solid silver coffee set. Thanking them all for their unselfish support, William Graham then recounted the early days of the company and its subsequent progress.

Aided by the stalwart A. E. Webster, Graham had indeed built up a highly successful company—despite the numerous difficulties which had attended its inception. Yet the heady days of the twenties—when he knew practically every employee by name—undoubtedly gave him the greatest pleasure. Latterly, he had made no secret of the fact that he sometimes thought the company was growing too big—and was genuinely hurt when a conductor failed to recognise him. Just prior to World War II he had sailed to the Isle of Wight aboard his beloved Norwegian cutter *Ørn*, but had been prevented from returning to Poole Harbour by rough weather. He was instead taken to Southampton aboard a friend's launch, where he disembarked at the Docks. There he had boarded a Dennis Ace bound for the Central Station and had announced to the conductor that all was well, since he was the Managing Director. Taking in the salt-stained yachting clothes, the conductor replied, 'Yes, I see Sir—and I'm the Chairman. Pay up!' 'The interests of the company seem to be in good hands,' William Graham murmured to his startled companions, 'perhaps I should now spend a little more time at sea.'

The retirement was to prove well-timed. William Graham's brand of benevolent avuncularity, which many employees of the thirties have cause to remember with freely expressed gratitude, now seemed as anachronistic as had been his method for dealing with disputes at depot level. At each, an elected Traffic Committee met—often at midnight, after the last bus had returned—and the general manager would personally attend. One of the Netley Traffic Committee members recalls:

> Before the war, Mr. Graham used to drive up from Bournemouth in his red Daimler and park outside the little hut 'over-the-wall'. The meetings were held in his car. We weren't members of a trade union then; we'd formed what was called the Traffic Staff, to discuss any grievances—and what Mr. Barnes couldn't grant us we ask Mr. Graham for. In the car he used to say he'd give us all we asked, but it seldom materialised. We said what a good gentleman he was—and he was, but realised we weren't getting very far. Yet he was a fine man: he did it all so nicely!

The Founder's retirement was short: he died at his home, Old Pines in Ferndown on 12 May 1947—without being told of a dispute which had brought his beloved company its first strike.

LABOUR RELATIONS

In some ways, Albert Webster's reward for his loyalty to the company was double edged: the fleet was in urgent need of pruning at a time when replacement vehicles were extremely scarce, whilst re-employed servicemen brought with them new ideals and a desire for negotiating powers of a kind unthinkable during the Graham era. (See Appendix D: 2.) Whereas, prior to the war, union members were comparatively few, membership had now gone up by leaps and bounds. Because of its association with the Southern Railway, the company decided to recognise and deal exclusively with the road transport section of the National Union of Railwaymen, which was now attempting to wrest better conditions for busmen from the National Council for the Omnibus Industry.

Yet for many of the more militant members of the union, their representatives' claims were being made upon far too narrow a front. Against a background of general unrest in the industry, particularly in the North and Midlands, a meeting of local officials at Parkstone on 16 February 1947 decided that a 24-hour stoppage would take place unless several outstanding grievances at local level were met. These were 'a long standing claim by clerical and supervisory staff for appropriate trade union recognition; a review of tours operators' conditions of service and of maintenance engineers', unchanged since 1942; a fortnight's holiday; time and a half on Sundays; a 44-hour week already enjoyed by local municipal omnibus crews' and several other points which the branch secretary noted 'with extreme regret' that the union had failed to take up with the company.

On 10 March, the secretary of the Bournemouth branch announced that, in the light of no further developments, an initial 24-hour stoppage would take place within the next ten days. Despite a protestation from the general secretary of the NUR that token stoppages would do great harm to the union, this took place, without prior notice, five days later and Wilts & Dorset crews joined in: it was an action designed to jostle the union as much as the respective companies. Throughout that day there were unprecedented scenes at Bournemouth and Southampton. Wilts & Dorset buses driven from Salisbury by inspectors were harassed by pickets and left town by unusual routes, whilst at Southampton, two buses were 'captured' and had to be rescued and return light to Salisbury under police escort. A report—inaccurate, it eventually transpired—that a Wilts & Dorset inspector had been dismissed for refusing to drive a bus, exacerbated the situation and an incredible day was brought to a close with the despatch from Bournemouth to Salisbury of a dramatic telegram which read, 'Tell Sparks not to worry. He will have our full support.'

Union reassurance that their grievances would be actively pursued staved off a further withdrawal of labour until 1 July 1947, when five hundred employees at Bournemouth decided to override the decision of other local NUR delegates to defer strike action until the outcome of negotiations at national level. All Hants & Dorset services from The Square were suspended and this time Royal Blue employees decided to participate. Feelings again ran high and police escorts were provided at the Pavilion Garage, where there were determined efforts to immobilise touring coaches. At one stage no fewer than eight stood on the parking lot behind the bus station with all their tyres deflated and bus drivers from other depots—including those of Wilts & Dorset, who had not joined in on this occasion, were persuaded to 'put up a blank' and return light. The following day, the strike spread to the Netley depot and pickets at Woolston talked the crews of Fareham and Gosport buses into refusing to take up passengers before Park Gate.

Both depots returned to work on 4 July, but the crews concerned announced their intention to withdraw from duty on Sundays until the results of the national negotiations were known.

The general manager's initial reaction—fashioned as it was by times which had now passed—had been a predictably autocratic document which hinted darkly of 'absenteeism without cause' and 'disciplinary action'. Yet, within weeks, the veracity of the crews had clearly made an impression upon him and he subsequently announced that there was 'no question of disciplinary action being taken against the men'. When personal prestige might have seemed better preserved by intractability, it was indeed a courageous decision and did much to take the heat out of the immediate situation.

POST-WAR RECOVERY

Meanwhile, plans proceeded apace to restore the company to a peace-time footing. A small excursion programme was restored in April 1946 and in the following year, the Isle of Wight tour was restarted with new Bristol coaches. These were to spend three seasons upon the island, after which the Southern Vectis Omnibus Company Ltd agreed to provide the vehicles for the island-circular section of the tour—and Hants & Dorset's garage at Yarmouth was closed.

Extensive dredging operations at the mouth of Poole Harbour delayed the re-opening of the ferry service until 12 July 1946, when a Leyland 'LT5A' saloon restarted the 'amphibious' route to Swanage. There was now a carnival mood abroad: the general post-war gaiety, in the years before television pinned father to the fireside, led to a heavy demand for coach tours and long country bus rides 'just for the hell of it'. The setting up of new light industries and a marked shift of population led to increased stage carriage traffic also and, as new Bristol and Leyland buses became available, so vehicle mileage began to build up to something approaching an all-time record. The several adjustments made in this period of expansion included the replacement of the old completely pre-printed Bell Punch ticket with the insert Setright system (subsequently superseded by the continuous-roll Speed Setright), a joint running agreement with Wilts & Dorset on the Winchester and Andover route, plans for a new bus station at Woolston and, on 31 March 1948, the transfer of the company's registered office from the Royal Mews to the Pavilion Garage at 8 Bath Road. For a decade, the general manager's office window was to present an unparalleled vista of Bournemouth Pier and the blue waters of Poole Bay.

CHAPTER NINE

STATE OWNERSHIP

THE BRITISH TRANSPORT COMMISSION

ON 1 JANUARY 1948, the Southern Railway—together with its assets—was nationalised and became the basis for British Railways' Southern Region. Thus over one-third of Hants & Dorset's share capital became state property. In September, Thomas Tilling Ltd agreed to sell their interest and during the year ending 31 December 1949, the British Transport Commission acquired the remainder (save 2) of the privately held Ordinary shares at an equivalent price per share. (See Appendix B: 2 & 4.) With the acquisition of the Preference shares, the BTC became owners of virtually the entire share capital, but although the directors were thereafter appointed by the BTC, the structure of management remained unaltered. In common with other Tilling companies, Hants & Dorset Motor Services Ltd retained its title and the Tilling Group Management Board continued to control the overall policy of the company.

This arrangement kept licensing and day-to-day affairs in the hands of those who knew the area intimately, which in turn meant that the company's resources would be deployed profitably for the next twenty years; a profit which now accrued to the state. One of the newly appointed directors was Albert Webster, who enjoyed this additional distinction until he retired from his post as general manager in October 1949.

The vacant directorship and post of general manager were taken up by George H. Napthine, who came to Bournemouth from Westcliff-on-Sea Motor Services Ltd.

A TIME OF CHANGE

The remaining petrol-engined vehicles were now phased out of service. Towards the end, some of the twenty year old Leyland 'Titans'—their autovacs stained bright pink by rationed commercial grade petrol—were still capable of spritely performances and several drivers regularly did their best to claim one for the day's shift.

The year 1950 also saw the end of fuel rationing, but before the general rejoicing had died, the Finance Act had forced up the price of petroleum products. This proved to be the straw which finally overburdened the company's attempts to cope with increased costs across the board, without adjusting the fares structure. Despite the difficulties which had attended war-time operations, this had remained unaltered for over twenty years—indeed, most fares were actually lower than they had been during the twenties. A general increase of fares was sanctioned and this came into effect on 11 December 1950. Since that date, the inflationary spiral—with which we are all too familiar—has caused frequent application to the licensing authority for permission to put fares at a realistic level in terms of the contemporary cost of operation.

Among employees, earlier disenchantment with their union led to a search for what was considered a more appropriate representational body to cater for the needs of those employed in the bus industry. It manifested itself in the formation, from among the ranks of the company, of the National Busworkers' Association, with its headquarters at Southampton. Several thousand busworkers joined—including many employed by Bristol Tramways—but the company, backed by strong words from no less a personage than Minister of Labour Alfred Robens, steadfastly refused to deal with any union other than the NUR. Despite support for the association from Colonel Crosthwaite-Eyre, MP, a prolonged strike and the tragic accidental death of a member on picket duty, it remained unyielding. There was much hard bargaining: concessions were made on both sides and there was a gradual return to the happier relationship of pre-war days, but the dissolution of the NBA is still looked upon wistfully by some of the more mature employees.

VEHICULAR DEVELOPMENTS

The early fifties saw the expansion of Esso's Fawley Refinery complex, with greatly increased contract work—and returns for this kind of traffic reached an all-time high. During the next decade further stage carriage services were acquired: in August 1952 Easson's Woolston–Hedge End route: in June 1955 Hursley Motor Services' routes to Farley, Southampton and Winchester; and in July 1959 Bere Regis & District Motor Services relinquished four routes in the Poole, Bere Regis and Dorchester area.

There were several developments in the vehicular design field during George Napthine's period as general manager. Firstly, some three years after pioneering work by Southampton Corporation at the behest of the Ministries of Health and Transport, Hants & Dorset fitted a Bristol double decker with an experimental heating and ventilating system devised at Southampton University by Wing Commander T. R. Cave-Browne-Cave, and placed it in service in 1953. Piped heat from the engine raised the temperature of air admitted through twin radiators. During the summer, this air was exhausted through side vents without admission to the saloons or was mixed with cold air as required. A Bristol Lodekka so-fitted followed in 1956 and the Cave-Browne-Cave system became standard for all company double deckers delivered between 1961 and 1967.

Fired by the success of open-topped double deckers at Westcliff, G. H. Napthine decided to employ similar vehicles upon the Sandbanks route. These were designed by William Barnes, the bodyshop superintendent at Southampton's Winchester Road premises and were full-fronted vehicles erected upon the wooden frames of elderly buses. The prototype, Leyland 'Titan' No 1005, entered service in April 1952 and was followed by many more on

Bristol chassis. They also saw service on the Gosport–Lee-on-Solent route—particularly during the Coronation Fleet Review—and on Southampton Docks tours, until the last was sold in 1971. Rebodied convertible open-toppers, which left their roofs suspended from the rafters of the Grosvenor Square garage during the summer, were also introduced but proved less successful.

A more lasting innovation began two years earlier, in August 1950, when Leyland 'Cub' coach No 644 was refitted as a service bus with a power-operated door. Thereafter, there has been a continual programme of converting elderly coaches into stage carriage vehicles for one-man operation, facilitated from 1960 onwards by the specification of power-operated doors for all new coaches. Accordingly, since the policy was introduced, comparatively fewer saloon buses have been purchased new and the subsequent saving has been ploughed back into the provision of better facilities.

IMPROVED BUS STATIONS

Further changes stemmed from a 1953 decision to extend and improve existing facilities for both company and the travelling public. Top priority was given to the complete modernisation of the famous bus station at The Square. When work began, the Bournemouth fleet was housed and maintained at three garages: Norwich Avenue, St Michael's Road and the Pavilion Garage, whilst the head office staff was split between Norwich Avenue and 8 Bath Road. The enlarged station would bring all these departments together under the one roof. Designed by the Tilling group's architect, Mr A. A. Briggs, the new office block, marshalling and control areas, maintenance bays and ancillary facilities, together with the enlarged Royal Blue coach station beneath, were constructed during a two-year period commencing in March 1957. As early as the summer of 1958, it became clear that on a typical day, Hants & Dorset's upper ground floor station could handle 60,000 passenger arrivals and departures, and 1,600 vehicle movements. This was made possible by the provision of a total platform length of 612ft and a parking layout which ensured a one-way traffic flow. Beneath, from the lower ground floor station, Royal Blue Express coaches and Associated Motorways were now moving as many as 18,000 long-distance passengers per day. Yet the layout of this unique building occasionally causes slight confusion among those unfamiliar with the terrain: the author, walking beside the Royal Blue exit at the rear of the station, was recently approached by an elderly lady with a request for help in locating the bus for Poole. On being informed that the Hants & Dorset buses could be reached by the staircase, the good lady gave a snort of disbelief and remarked facetiously that the bus on which she'd arrived from Poole 'certainly hadn't gone up any stairs, thank you very much' and hurried off in search of less addled guidance.

The headquarters offices moved into the top floor suite of the administration block in September 1958. Although 8 Bath Road had ceased to be the registered office of the company, the garage was retained as a winter base for coaches and open-topped buses, together with a ground floor booking office for tours and excursions. The historic Royal Mews in Norwich Avenue and the St Michael's Road garage were closed.

George Napthine retired in the spring of 1958. He was succeeded as general manager by Douglas W. Morison, who like Albert Webster, had a record of long service with the company and was promoted from traffic manager. He actively pursued the modernisation programme and further work was carried out at Ringwood, Lymington, Fareham and Southampton. Expansion at Fareham followed the demolition of the old Wesleyan Chapel, whilst the updating of Southampton Bus Station, completed in the late sixties, swallowed bomb-torn Birmingham Street and introduced the first 'saw-tooth' high-density departure bays.

INTO EUROPE

Douglas Morison was to take a keen interest in the tours and excursions department. Weekly travel film shows for the public were introduced and given in the headquarters committee room, which had been specially adapted as a small theatre. In March 1960, he summed up the role of the department within the framework of the company's operations:

> The fares structure for day tours is largely controlled by competitive influences, but where co-ordination between competitors can be obtained, the fares level chosen is usually equal to or slightly above that for the stage carriage bus return fare, or the railway day excursion fare. Apart from the need to battle with competition by road or rail, day tour fares are governed, as in the end all other fares are, by the law of supply and demand.
>
> Extended holiday tours are a specialised operation, and the fares have to cover hotel accommodation, meals and other items as well as the actual road journey element; the mileage varies considerably according to the nature of the tour, and does not have any direct relationship to the fare, which is usually fixed according to the duration of the tour. The charges are based having regard to the need for making an overall profit on an activity which is a distinct and separate branch of the Company's business.
>
> Private hire, both of the coach and bus fleet, is an important source of revenue, but is subject to intense competition. Quality of vehicles and service will be an aid to obtaining business in the face of competition, but a Company with a reputation and high standard of maintenance of vehicles and buildings will always be subject to undercutting by smaller operators with cheaper overhead costs.
>
> The large operator must therefore cut his private hire costs to a very fine limit, and regard private hire of vehicles not as an end in itself, but as a means of keeping vehicles occupied, thereby spreading overhead costs, during otherwise idle periods of stage carriage or tours operation. The integration of bus and coach fleets as far as is practicable is an essential to the lowering of costs and the maintenance of a low and attractive fares or private hire rates structure.

For many years the new general manager had nursed a regret that Hants & Dorset—despite provision for such work being written into the articles of association way back in 1916—were not represented among Continental tours operators: he now set out to remedy the situation. Initial experience was culled in the early sixties from the Southern Ireland tour: passengers were originally flown from Lulsgate Airport, Bristol to Dublin, where they joined a Dublin-based Hants & Dorset coach for a circular tour to Killarney. This was extended to become an all-Ireland circular, and to gain 'cross channel' experience the coach which left Bournemouth went 'right through' on the ferry from Liverpool to Belfast.

It was a party of horticulturists from Totton who provided the company with its first European adventure. On Saturday, 20 April 1963, with a courier from Thomas Cook & Son and L. T. Cole of the Southampton Tours department aboard, Bristol coach No 880 was driven on to the SS *Artevelde* at Dover for the start of an 8-day tour of the Dutch bulbfields. Weekend trips to Paris followed, and an expanding programme now includes 4–12-day tours to Austria, Switzerland, the Italian Lakes, Alsace, the Austrian Tyrol and the Schwarzwald, using the Thoresen Ferries from Southampton as the bridge to the Continent. Upwards of thirty different extended tours in Britain and Europe are now offered throughout a long summer season, whilst foreign language brochures are also issued to cater for the growing number of Continental visitors to Bournemouth and district.

WILTS & DORSET

In 1962, a new Transport Act dismembered the British Transport Commission. Hants & Dorset and the other companies administered by Tillings Transport (BTC) Ltd—now renamed 'the Tilling Association Ltd'—were placed under the ultimate control of the Transport Holding Company, which had been set up under the Act. Although financial links with the Railways Board were severed by this adjustment, British Railways officials Arthur C. J. Payne and Percy A. White retained their representative directorships of Hants & Dorset Motor Services Ltd and further British Rail officers have since taken their places upon the board.

On 3 April 1964, the general manager of Wilts & Dorset Motor Services Ltd, David Deacon, resigned and joined the Tilling Association board. Hants & Dorset's general manager, Douglas Morison, then became general manager of Wilts & Dorset also, thus setting in motion a long-expected merger of the two fleets. The following year, upon the retirement from the board of Thomas Gailey, David Deacon became chairman of Hants & Dorset—and the registered office of Wilts & Dorset and its subsidiary Venture Ltd was transferred to The Square, Bournemouth. From 1 January 1969, Wilts & Dorset officially became 'Hants & Dorset Motor Services Ltd trading as Wilts & Dorset', but whilst Hants & Dorset's services are worked under the jurisdiction of the South Eastern Traffic Commissioners, Wilts & Dorset's remained under the Western. Although the fleetname and Tilling red and cream livery continued in use, from that date all new Wilts & Dorset buses carried Bournemouth registrations. In 1971, a complete renumbering of the combined fleets disclosed that Wilts & Dorset was indeed the 'Northern Area' of Hants & Dorset Motor Services Ltd. Thus, the way was paved for the subsequent demise of the Wilts & Dorset title, although by virtue of an NBC directive, a pale pastel reminder of that company will survive upon all Hants & Dorset buses, following the adoption of NBC's poppy red livery in place of the traditional green and cream.

SHAMROCK & RAMBLER

Shamrock & Rambler Coaches Ltd, together with its subsidiary Charlie's Cars (Bournemouth) Ltd, was acquired by the Tilling Association Ltd in 1966. On 8 July, Hants & Dorset directors David Deacon, Douglas Morison and Thomas Pruett were appointed directors of both companies and management of their affairs was transferred to The Square. The familiar Shamrock & Rambler coaches—each individually named—stemmed from a business started in 1888 and motorised by that respected Bournemouth citizen, William J. Whitelock, in April 1913. During the thirties, Shamrock & Rambler had operated an express service between Bournemouth and London in competition with Royal Blue and—later—opened offices at Southampton and Brighton. Both their orange livery and the 'plum and spilt milk' of Charlie's Cars survives at the time of writing: the Southampton-based fleet

OPERATING RESOURCES: DEPLOYMENT OF STAFF AND VEHICLES AS AT 30 MARCH 1967

(NOT INCLUDING HEAD OFFICE ADMINISTRATION, CENTRAL WORKSHOPS OR OVERHAUL STAFF)

Code No	*Location*	*Function*	*Vehicles*	*Drivers*	*Conductors*	*Super-visory*	*Clerical*	*Main-tenance*	*Total Staff*	*Official in Charge*
1	Poole	PD*	79	131	121	8	15	33	308	OS
2	Wareham	O	1	2	2	—	—	—	4	—
2A	Bere Regis	O	1	2	—	—	—	—	2	—
3	Bournemouth	PD*	87	128	112	18	20	55	333	OS
4	Swanage	O	3	8	—	—	—	—	8	I
5	Blandford	O	6	8	6	—	—	—	14	—
6	Shaftesbury	O	1	2	2	—	—	—	4	—
7	Ringwood	SD*	24	33	23	2	4	8	70	DI
8	Lymington	SD*	21	40	26	3	3	12	84	DI
9	Southampton	PD*	101	147	120	15	38	81	403	OS
10	Lyndhurst	O	5	8	5	—	1	—	13	—
10A	Nomansland	O	1	2	—	—	—	—	2	—
11	Bishops Waltham	O	3	7	6	—	—	—	13	—
12	Hythe	O	8	12	9	—	—	—	21	—
13	Romsey	O	2	4	2	—	1	—	6	—
14	Winchester	PD*	21	33	25	4	5	9	76	OS
15	Eastleigh	SD*	18	29	29	3	3	9	73	DI
16	Petersfield	O	3	6	2	—	—	—	8	—
17	Fareham	PD*	39	72	56	8	8	24	168	OS
18	Woolston	SD*	19	29	30	2	4	8	73	DI
19	Gosport	O	4	6	6	—	—	—	12	—
			447	709	582	63	102	239	1,695	

PD: Principal depot; O: Outstation; SD Small depot; *Vehicles maintained here identified by Colour Code in 1955–1971 Series. OS: Operating Superintendent; I: Inspector: DI: Depot Inspector.

This table is based upon an official Hants & Dorset document and represents deployment before Wilts & Dorset became an integral part of the Company

Page 173 (*above*) 1938: H & D's first Bristols (made by a Tilling company) were its last buses bodied by Brush (BET) and marked the ascendency of the Tilling group; (*below*) Doodlebug weather: on an equally grey day in 1944, all-grey Leyland E332 stands harnessed to its gas-producing trailer at Fareham Bus Station

Page 174 (*above*) Three general managers of Hants & Dorset at the founder's retirement party: William Graham 1916–45 (centre), Albert Webster 1945–49 (2nd left) and Douglas Morison 1958–71 (3rd left). W. George (secretary), R. Longman (managing director) and P. Pelling (engineer) complete the group; (*below*) March 1958: the extensive reconstruction of Bournemouth Bus Station

having been numbered within the Hants & Dorset series and joined by company coaches repainted in Shamrock & Rambler livery. Further Shamrock & Rambler vehicles based upon the Isle of Wight were placed under the control of Southern Vectis Omnibus Company Ltd.

PROVINCIAL

The National Bus Company (incorporated by statute under the Transport Act of 1968—and successor to the Transport Holding Company) celebrated its first birthday on 1 January 1970 by purchasing the bus operations of the Provincial Traction Company Ltd, the parent of Gosport & Fareham Omnibus Company. The private hire and contract work of Provincial were immediately placed under the control of Hants & Dorset Motor Services Ltd, but the position of Gosport & Fareham Omnibus Company, protected as it is by statute, is slightly different. Douglas Morison was appointed managing director and the registered office was transferred to The Square, Bournemouth, but the legal ownership remains unchanged and for the forseeable future the fleet will retain its identity and continue to operate the services in its area. The arrangement quickly proved mutually beneficial: Daimler Fleetline double deckers originally intended for Gosport & Fareham were exchanged before entry into service for Hants & Dorset-bound Bristol saloons, the requirements of both having changed since placement of the orders.

DIFFICULT TIMES

The Act which brought the National Bus Company into being also introduced new legislation restricting bus drivers' hours. This came into effect on Sunday, 15 March 1970: more than 5½ hours driving without a 30-minute break was thereafter prohibited. Furthermore, within a set 14-hour day, no driver was permitted to drive for more than 10 hours, thus the practice of maintaining the timetable by offering drivers considerable overtime and opportunities to work rest days, became unworkable

L

overnight. Neither the company nor the crews found this to be financially advantageous. The most immediate result was that Hants & Dorset found itself short of drivers: throughout March and April many departures were cancelled or curtailed on a day-to-day basis if sickness further reduced the available pool. At the Southampton depot alone, 2,700 miles per week were lost and it was estimated that a further 29 drivers would be required to maintain the existing Southampton area schedules. An immediate recruitment drive was set in motion, but inevitably the suspension of some services led to permanent pruning and outright cancellation.

This inescapable sequence of events almost certainly contributed towards a noticeable increase in the use of alternative means of transport within the company area and finally upset valiant efforts by the management—at times bordering upon wizardry—to contain what was part of a national tendency among bus companies towards an annual deficit. The returns at 31 December 1970 showed that Hants & Dorset employed an average of 2,773 persons throughout that difficult year with an aggregate remuneration amounting to £3,329,073—a bill swollen by the wages of new staff, employed to maintain schedules less extensive than those previously operated and subscribed to by fewer passengers. Not surprisingly, the returns also disclosed that the company had made its first ever loss.

One helpful factor in the intensified search for economies proved to be the new relationship with Wilts & Dorset. An investigation into the areas of overlap led to a reorganisation of services in the Avon Valley. From February 1972, Ringwood reverted to its pre-war role of outstation and Fordingbridge became the co-axial point. In the Eastern Area, Woolston ceased to function as a depot and departures are now made from a series of joint Hants & Dorset and Southampton Corporation bays.

FUTURE PROSPECTS

On 31 December 1971, Douglas Morison left the company. A spontaneous show of their regard by Bournemouth crews, which attended his departure, reflected his popularity and rapport with the employees.

The new general manager is Peter C. Hunt, ex-general manager of the Yorkshire Traction Company Ltd. On 1 April 1972, he also became one of the eight chief general managers of the National Bus Company, with personal responsibility for Hants & Dorset, Wilts & Dorset, Gosport & Fareham, Southern Vectis and the Thames Valley & Aldershot Omnibus Company Ltd. He has taken up the reins at a time when the future direction of the industry as a whole is obscure. There is little doubt that the road ahead will be difficult: local government grants may well keep in being several of the more sparsely populated routes, but will do nothing towards the restoration of the company's financial health. Now that the NBC controls the affairs of the ex-BET group, whose services—by and large—operate through more densely populated areas, it may well prove necessary to enlist aid from that quarter. There are signs that in Hants & Dorset's case this is already taking place: 33 Leyland 'Panther' saloons of 1967 vintage, transferred from the ex-BET 'Maidstone & District' at the close of 1971, although paid-for, represent a considerable saving against the cost of a similar number of brand-new vehicles.

But, as John Hibbs points out in his . . . *History of British Bus Services*, 'It was for the passenger that the industry came into existence and it will be the passenger who will have the last word: it is he to whom transport should be the servant.' Just who such passengers will be and—more important—how many, depends to a large extent upon the deliberations of the committee formulating the South Hampshire Plan. The area between and including Southampton and Gosport—always one of Hants & Dorset's best money spinners—probably holds the long-term key to the company's future as a separate entity. Over a twenty-year period, even without a Solent City as envisaged by Professor Colin Buchanan, the population is expected to rise by 290,000. If new light industries are established centrally, there will be increased demand for short-haul stage carriage services of the kind presently operated by municipalities.

On the other hand, it is expected that there will be four times as many private cars in the area. Apart from restricting the company's share of the increased traffic, private car ownership on such a scale could make nonsense of the timetables in the resulting congestion. Running a bus company under such difficulties will be no job for the faint-hearted: nothing short of a system of 'buses-only' at the terminal points, priority through-ways on the approaches, legislation to restrict the daily use of private cars and a reduction in fuel bills would seem likely to prevent Hants & Dorset and its sister companies becoming a drain upon the state. All these measures would be beyond the powers of company management, yet without them their task would seem insuperable. Although such controls would be controversial, they are not beyond implementation by the ultimate benefactors.

It seems clear that the role found for Hants & Dorset Motor Services Ltd by the South Hampshire Advisory Committee and the measures taken to protect that role, will also have far reaching effects upon the company's ability to maintain its services in the more distant areas of Hampshire, Dorset and Wiltshire. Without such services, man's regard for his fellow-beings would need to improve apace. Yet the warning is there—rural railway lines have gone and been replaced by bus services, some of which have themselves proved unprofitable and been withdrawn.

However, one firmly established service—which has a distinctly historic flavour about it—actually makes use of the track bed of an old railway line. This was the original 'Castleman's Corkscrew', closed to passenger traffic in 1964, a section subsequently being used to re-route the Burley and Lymington road away from the notorious Wilverley Post cross roads. The new road passes under the 'railway' bridge carrying the A35 and sweeps the traffic at wheel depth beneath the platform of the old Holmsley Station building. Periodically, Hants & Dorset's Limited Stop Service X 17 'steams' through the station were the LSWR trains once stopped for Francis Graham's passengers. Somewhere, the old man must be smiling!

CHAPTER TEN

ROLLING STOCK

MAKES AND TYPES

SEVERAL MAKES of vehicle have been mentioned in the foregoing text. The following summary, which does not include service vehicles, is a complete list of types numbered within the Hants & Dorset fleet up to the time of writing. Greater attention has been paid to those vehicles operated prior to World War II.

AEC

B, Y and YC Introduced between 1919 and 1924, these were a mixed bag of second-hand chassis fitted with various makes of charabanc and omnibus bodywork. All were powered by Tylor JB4 40–45hp engines.

662 'REGAL' Six coaches with Duple 'crash-proof' bodywork, acquired from Royal Blue in 1935. They were 26ft long and fitted with AEC 6cyl petrol engines.

762 'Q' type Four coaches, acquired as above, fitted with side-mounted AEC engines, Wilson pre-selector gearboxes and equal axle loadings. Nicknamed 'Jumbos'.

661 'REGENT' One Willowbrook-bodied double-decker purchased for evaluation in 1935 and three second-hand Tilling-bodied examples with open staircases purchased in 1947.

6811A 'REGENT' Six double-deckers with Northern Counties bodywork, purchased to off-set Bristol K double-deckers on loan to the London Transport Executive in 1949.

2MU3 'RELIANCE' Three Shamrock & Rambler coaches with

Duple 'Britannia' bodies transferred to the H & D fleet in 1969. They were built in 1961.

ADC (*Associated Daimler Company*)

424 Eight normal-control convertible coaches acquired from Royal Blue in 1935. Although allotted company numbers, they were immediately offered for sale.

AJS

PILOT (OVERTYPE) One saloon omnibus, acquired in 1931, with Eaton bodywork. A product of the well-known motor cycle manufacturer, the bus was fitted with a 6cyl engine developing 54bhp.

Albion

PH 49 'VICTOR' One coach, fitted with Wadham bodywork, acquired from Tourist in 1935. Designed for country-lane work, it was only 6ft 2in wide with single seats on the near side of the gangway. 4cyl engine.

PX 65 'Valkyrie' One coach, also with Wadham body, acquired from Rob Roy Coaches in 1935. A forward-control model, it was fitted with a 4cyl petrol engine.

Bedford

WLB Two 20-seat coaches acquired in 1935. The Duple-bodied example came from Rob Roy Coaches, whilst that by Wilmott was acquired from Billie's Coaches. The 6cyl petrol engines developed 26·3hp RAC.

OB Seven Beadle bodied 20-seat saloons (1949) and 3 Duple coaches (1950), with petrol engines originally.

SB 5 Three coaches of 1963 vintage, Duple bodied and in Shamrock & Rambler livery, transferred to the H & D list in 1969.

VAM 14 and 70 Fifteen saloon buses with Leyland or Bedford oil engines and Strachan or Willowbrook coachwork—5 with space for 25 standing passengers. Delivered 1966–8.

VAL Three-axle 49/52-seat Duple bodied coaches in Hants & Dorset and Shamrock & Rambler liveries (from 1969).

Berliet

VMB Two saloon omnibuses acquired from Phipps in 1926. Originally built in France as '*camionettes de 1,800kgs, avec 4 cylindres verticaux*', the chassis had been lengthened at Thornycroft's Woolston shipyard and Paine & Frampton bodies fitted.

Bristol

K Introduced in 1938, the purchase of this chassis (intended for double deckers) represented the ascendancy of the Tilling interest within the company. The first 23 were bodied by Brush—and marked the swansong of BAT policy. Thereafter, all peace-time deliveries were bodied by the Tilling-controlled Eastern Coachworks Ltd. Those purchased prior to World War II (K5Gs) were fitted with Gardner 5cyl oil engines. So, too, were 4 utility bodied examples delivered in 1942, but 7 further vehicles which entered service in 1944–5 were powered by AEC 6cyl oil units—and designated K6A. Post-war examples were fitted with a more shapely low-profile radiator; Gardner, AEC and 6cyl Bristol engines (type K6B)—and Series II lowbridge bodies by ECW. The 136 delivered were by far the largest batch of similar vehicles operated by Hants & Dorset and were extremely popular with the maintenance crews. Thirty-nine were hired to the London Transport Executive (1948–50), being delivered new to the Godstone and Watford depots.

KS At 27ft, this type was one foot longer than the K. Seventeen with ECW lowbridge bodies were purchased (1950–1), the last six with 8ft wide bodies on the 7ft 6in chassis—and a white steering wheel to warn the drivers.

KSW 8ft wide (chassis and bodywork) version of the KS. Fourteen lowbridge and thirty-eight highbridge examples with ECW bodies delivered (1951–3).

L Introduced in 1938, thirty-seven Beadle-bodied saloons were delivered over a two-year period. Gardner 5cyl oil engines were fitted. Post-war examples had the same radiator as the contemporary K. Twelve ECW-bodied saloons and thirty-nine coaches delivered 1947–50, with Gardner, AEC and Bristol oil engines.

LL The first 30ft vehicles operated: two dual purpose saloons

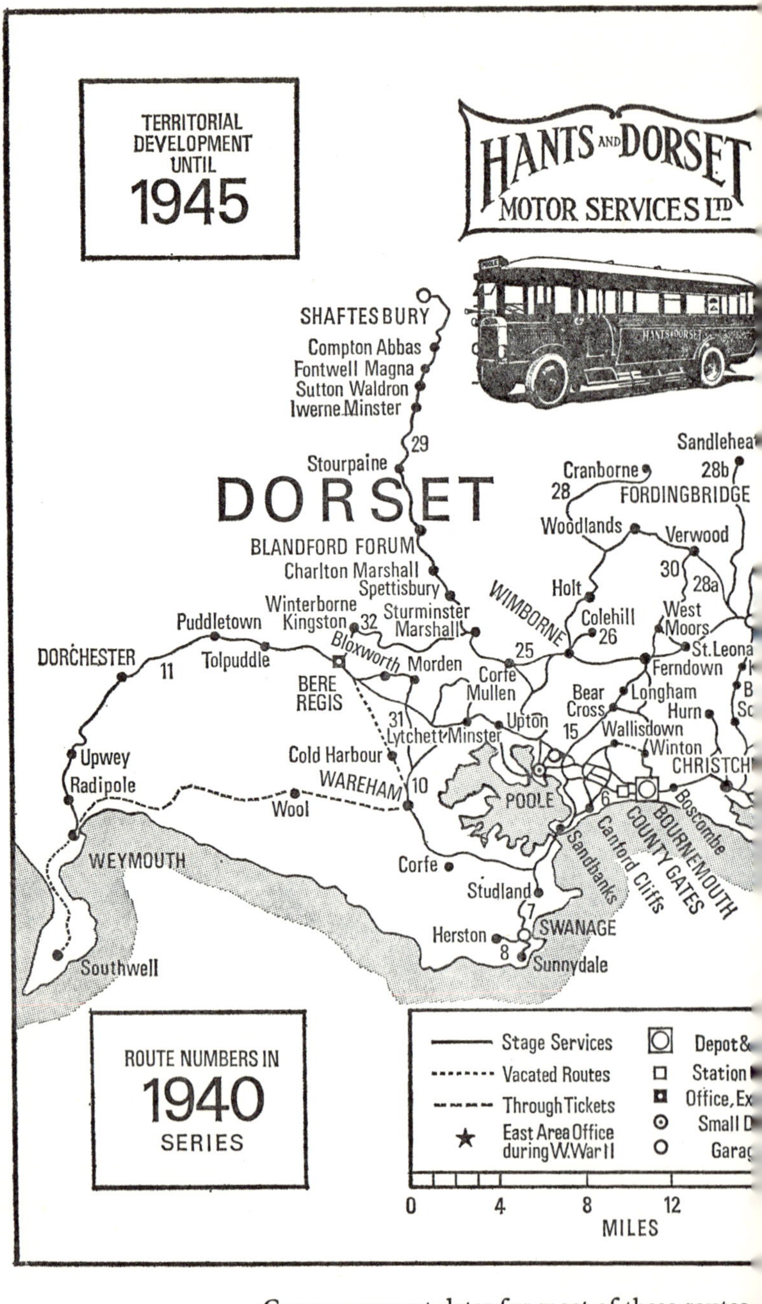

Commencement dates for most of these routes

on pages 78, 102, 106, 109, 118, 128, 131 and 135

with Portsmouth Aviation bodies and Gardner engines, seven with ECW bodies and Bristol engines (1950–2), together with five full-fronted 8ft wide ECW coaches with white steering wheel to remind the drivers.

LWL 8ft wide version of the LL. One dual purpose saloon (Gardner engined) with Portsmouth Aviation and 6 coaches (Bristol) with full-fronted ECW coachwork.

LS Underfloor-engined 'light saloon' chassis. Twenty ECW saloons (1953–7), plus a further four converted from ex-Southern Vectis coaches in 1968. Fifteen ECW coaches delivered 1953–7.

LD H & D's first Lodekka—the ECW/Bristol double decker which was low-height, yet dispensed with the side gangway layout upstairs and the step over which most passengers tripped downstairs—was delivered in April 1953. A further ninety-seven had been added by 1960, making it H & D's second most numerous type. Bristol or Gardner oil engines fitted.

LDL The first 30ft double decker, it was an extended version of the LD and was purchased in 1957 to gain experience in readiness for the operation of further 70-seat types.

MW Fourteen 'medium weight' saloons and 46 coaches—all with ECW bodies—delivered between 1958 and 1966.

FS Sixty-eight 'flat floor short' Lodekkas were purchased (1960–5). All have 60-seat ECW bodies and Bristol or Gardner engines.

FL Twelve 'flat floor long' Lodekkas with 70-seat ECW bodies (1961–2). Bristol or Gardner engines.

FLF 70-seat 'flat floor long, front entrance' Lodekka. Sixty-two delivered with ECW coachwork and Bristol, Gardner or Leyland engines (1965–7).

RELH 'Rear-engined' coaches, the first 36ft vehicles operated. Gardner engines and bodywork by ECW and Duple. Deliveries began in 1964.

RELL Saloon bus version of the RELH and the first Bristol/ECW buses licensed to carry 23 standing passengers in addition to those seated. Entered service 1968.

RESH Four 33ft coaches—a shortened version of the RELH, with Duple bodywork.

LH A completely revised 'lightweight horizontal' engined saloon, with—in Hants & Dorset's case—a 6·5 litre Leyland engine between the axles. Introduced in 1968.

VRT(SL) Hants & Dorset's first Bristol 'vertical rear (engine) transverse (-ly mounted)' ECW front entrance double deckers began work long after those of its sister companies. Deliveries commenced with the Gardner engined, shorter version in the winter of 1972–3.

Chevrolet

B, X, LM and LQ An assortment of these 14-seat saloons was acquired in 1930–1, whilst two examples were purchased new. All were fitted with 4cyl petrol units.

Daimler

Y Most Y type chassis were refurbished World War I lorries, which in turn had been developed from AEC's B type. Thus, Daimler spares were liberally applied to several of Hants & Dorset's AEC charabancs. Further Y type charabancs were acquired when the company established itself at Gosport in 1924, but the twelve Dodson-bodied 'Charabuses', purchased from Royal Blue in that same year, represent the company's best-known examples. The majority were fitted with the 40hp Silent Knight 4cyl double sleeve-valve engine.

CC A development of the Y, six Brush-bodied double-decked open-toppers—previously operated by BAT in London—were somewhat hastily purchased in 1927. Licences were withheld, however, and only 210 and 212 saw service.

CF 6 Seven coaches with Duple bodywork, acquired from Royal Blue in 1935 and once part of their fleet of express service coaches on the London route. The original Daimler sleeve-valve engines were removed by the company at the Shirley Road works and the chassis were refitted with AEC units in May and June of that year. New cross-members were also fitted whilst this work was carried out. They retained their Royal Blue livery and were sold in 1937.

CR G6 'FLEETLINE' Hants & Dorset's first rear-engined,

one-man-operated double deckers, they were diverted new and unregistered from Provincial in exchange for some equally mint Bristol saloons. The six vehicles involved are fitted with front-entrance bodywork by Roe.

DeDion Bouton

30–35hp Two charabancs with Knight bodies, acquired from Eugene Poulain in 1918. Both were fitted with DeDion 4cyl units and featured the Solex radiator system, which superficially resembled the Mercedes-Benz trademark. Behind the grille, a square-tipped fan fitted neatly inside two crescent-shaped bundles of tubes which were gathered at the top and bottom into small tanks—the water being fed in from the top. Maximum cooling and freedom from dust were claimed for the system by the makers. Both charabancs continued in service upon the County Gates–Sandbanks route until replaced by more suitable vehicles in 1919.

Dennis

3 and 4 TON Two omnibuses and three charabancs on spoked wheels and solid tyres, acquired from H. Tutt & Sons' Enterprise in 1924 and operated on stage carriage services in the Fareham and Gosport area, until replaced by Daimler 'Charabuses' and Leyland GH7 open toppers.

2 TON One 20-seat saloon omnibus acquired from Enterprise. It was fitted with Mackintosh NAP tyres at the front and solids at the rear, and served upon the Gosport, Fareham and Bishops Waltham route.

'ACE' Ten of these attractive 20-seat vehicles—bodied by Brush—were purchased for work in the country lanes of Dorset, the New Forest and the confines of Southampton Docks; duties for which their 40ft turning circle ideally suited them. These 1934 models were joined three years later by two further examples bodied by Mumford and diverted from Western and Southern National. The type was nicknamed 'Flying Pig'.

Ford

AA Three were acquired between 1932 and 1936. They were

basically 25cwt lorry chassis, uprated with improved 4cyl petrol engines and chosen by their original owners for their economical work-rate.

Gilford

168 OT One coach—Weymann-bodied—acquired from Royal Blue in 1935. Fitted with 6cyl petrol engine and prominent Westinghouse 'Gruss Air-Springs', designed to give maximum shock absorption and eliminate recoil. Although numbered by the company, it was immediately offered for sale.

Guy

OND, ONDF Four saloons with Guy bodywork (one with forward control) acquired in September 1930. Fitted with 4cyl petrol engines, they were used on the routes of their original owners until suitable replacements became available.

'ARAB I' Nine utility-bodied double-deckers delivered in 1942 and 1943, mainly for use in the Eastleigh area. All were fitted with Gardner 5cyl oil engines.

Karrier

ZX Developed from the earlier C and CY models, this was a two-tonner fitted with a 4cyl petrol engine and bodywork by Rowdon of Lyndhurst. It was Hants & Dorset's only example and was acquired from C. A. Croucher's 'Yellow Bus Service'.

Lancia

'PENTAIOTA' Six 4cyl and three 6cyl examples acquired in 1927. As mentioned in the text, most were originally purchased by competitors to run against company buses. Besides being fast, these saloons were—with their turning circle of 44ft 7in—highly manoeuvrable.

Leyland

N, G5 Already mentioned at some length in the text, the N and its derivative, the G5, were fitted with 4cyl petrol engines, cast steel tubular wheels and solid Avon tyes. The first—delivered in April 1919—carried a Kiddle charabanc body (for one year only) and was then fitted with a Dodson saloon. So, too, was the second, whilst the third carried a 28-seat Kiddle saloon body, featuring electric headlamps at the front of the roof. Twenty-five others were fitted with 34-seat Dodson 'CD 19' type saloon bodies from new. In 1923, six more received Beadle bodies (the Seventy class). They were later to receive pneumatic tyres.

SG9 Delivered in 1925, these saloons were the company's first half-cabs. The first two received Leyland 'Special' bodies, based upon the contemporary Crosville type. The remaining seven were bodied by Beadle, who fitted each with a luggage rack towards the front of the roof, reached by a ladder placed immediately behind the near-side front wheel. Leyland 4cyl petrol engines.

GH7 First delivered in 1926, these 20 Brush-bodied open toppers were the company's first new double deckers. Originally on solids, some were tried with Mackintosh NAP tyres, but all were eventually given pneumatics. The 4cyl Leyland engines developed 36hp, giving a top speed of 16mph.

PLSC 1 'LION', PLSC 3 '(LONG) LION' The first low-loading omnibus, delivered in 1926 (17 examples) was followed into service by the PLSC 3 model, which was only 1ft 2½in longer, but allowed space for four extra seats. Thirty-one saloons and two coaches, all with Leyland bodywork, were purchased over a two-year period. They were joined by one second-hand example and a similarly acquired shorter version. Both types were fitted with 4cyl petrol engines.

PLA 2 'LEVERET' Introduced in 1926, initially for service at Swanage, the Leveret was a scaled-down normal control version of the Lion and intended for use as a 20-seat one-man bus. All four had Leyland bodywork and 4cyl petrol engines developing 34bhp. Surprisingly, the floor level was almost 3in higher than that of the Lion.

PLSP 2 'LEVIATHAN' The last four examples of this type to leave the Leyland works were delivered in 1927. Large half-cab double-decked open-toppers, unconfirmed evidence suggests that they were bodied by Tilling, but in BAT style. In common with several double-deckers of the period, the spare wheel was carried beneath the staircase. The 4cyl Leyland engine developed 34·3bhp and with a little coaxing, 5·25 miles per gallon could be achieved. Each suffered badly from front wheel wobble.

TD 1, 2, 3, 3C, 4C, 4 'TITAN' Introduced at Southampton in 1928, the first eighteen examples of this outstanding double-decker were fitted with open-top bodies in BAT style by Short Brothers. The following year, they were followed by an open-staired covered-top version—six bodied by Beadle and six by Short. Leyland built the bodywork for the next batch, the first seven examples featuring the original radiator with top tank only. The remaining eight had the full radiator, and an oval enamelled picture of a Titan's face replaced the usual Leyland nameplate on the top tank. In January 1930, the first of twenty-five with enclosed bodies (by Leyland) were delivered and saw service throughout the company area. All the Titans received by August 1931 were the TD 1 model, fitted with 6cyl petrol engines and semi-floating rear axles. The following year came 11 TD 2 models bodied by Eastern Counties. These featured a more powerful 6cyl engine and a fully-floating rear axle. Fourteen further examples, bodied by Brush, incorporated minor improvements, the outwardly visible difference being the revised dumb irons. Between 1934–7, fifteen TD 3 and twenty-seven TD 4 Titans were purchased, all fitted with Brush bodywork. Five of the former were powered by Leyland 6cyl oil engines, whilst five petrol-engined examples featured the torque converter mentioned in Chapter Six. Twenty-one TD 4s were petrol powered—eighteen with converters—and the remainder oil. Both models sported a much larger, parallel-sided radiator; the TD 4 also being fitted with a revised braking system. The basic specification remained the same, however, and in consequence the long production run took £250 from the price of each vehicle.

TS 2, 3, 7, 8 'TIGER' As mentioned in Chapter Four, two TS 2 saloons were purchased for competitive work in 1929. One Duple-bodied coach and eight Strachan-bodied examples were acquired from Royal Blue and Tourist respectively in 1935. Two TS 3 'Tigers'—differing only in the position of the rear axle—were acquired with the latter. All had 6cyl petrol units. Twenty-four TS 7 models—with radiators in TD 3 style—were purchased new and fitted with Beadle coach bodies. A further example was bodied by Brush and exhibited at the 1935 Commercial Motor Show before entering service: all were petrol engined. In 1938, eight TS 8 oil-engined models were purchased, again with coach bodies by Beadle.

LT 1, 5, 5A 'LION' The first of twelve LT 1 saloons with Leyland bodywork was delivered in 1929. Another with a Brush body was acquired the following year. Leyland-bodied examples were known as the 'Popular' model and cost £1,545 complete. Eight Brush-bodied LT 5 Lions—delivered in 1932—were 1ft 8in longer and fitted with revised radiators. A much deeper radiator was a distinguishing feature of the nine LT 5A Lions—again bodied by Brush—purchased in 1935. A new Clayton-Lockheed hydraulic braking system was one of the more important improvements. All the Lions were powered by 4cyl petrol units.

KP 2, KPZ 1, 2, 4 'CUB' A Leyland demonstrator—fitted with a 6cyl Chrysler engine—was acquired in 1933. Four months later, a quartet of Brush-bodied Cubs with Leyland engines was purchased. Three further Cubs—now designated KPZ 1, but costing £80 less—followed in 1936. At the same time, three KPZ 2 models, with wheelbase 1ft 6in longer, received Beadle coach bodies which were a scaled-down version of those fitted to the Tigers. Two similar KPZ 4 coaches followed in 1939.

PD 1A 'TITAN' Seven double-deckers with lowbridge bodies by ECW and oil engines by Leyland, new in 1948.

PD 2/1 'TITAN' Six 'all-Leyland' highbridge models originally intended for shipment to South Africa in 1949, but collected from Southampton New Docks in grey undercoat and finished in company colours. Further vehicles intended to offset the Bristol deckers loaned to the LTE, they made the southern shore of Southampton Water their own territory for the next thirteen years.

PSU 3 'LEOPARD' Plaxton-bodied coaches, with underfloor engines, first delivered in 1970.

Page 191 Hants & Dorset scene, 1970: (*above*) Bristol REL saloon No 836 at Brook in the New Forest, with a thatched cottage and ubiquitous ponies to complete the picture

(*left*) Bristol FLF, No 1520 with Cave-Browne-Cave air intakes, passenger doors and engine all at the front. H & D were late to buy rear-engined double deckers

(*below*) a PSU 3 'Leopard' coach—new Leylands, after a twenty-one year absence

Page 192 Holmsley Station, the original destination for the forerunners of both Hants & Dorset and Royal Blue: (*above*) as Francis Graham knew it in the nineteenth Century; (*below*) Bristol FS Lodekka No 1444 passes 'through' the station in the summer of 1969

PSUR 1/1R 'PANTHER' Thirty-three Duple (Willowbrook)-bodied, rear-engined saloons (1967 vintage) acquired from Maidstone & District in 1971 and repainted in company colours: sixteen in Wilts & Dorset red.

Maudslay

4 TON One of these large charabancs was acquired from Trade Cars in 1920. It was basically a Subsidy A-type lorry chassis—right down to the towing hooks on the dumb irons—and fitted with a 40hp, 4cyl engine, disc wheels and solid tyres.

Milnes Daimler

28hp Two saloons acquired from the Canford Cliffs Motor Omnibus Company in 1918, the company's first real stage carriage vehicles. They were fitted with German Daimler engines with 4 cylinders cast in pairs, leather-covered cone clutch, and final drive by toothed rings on the inside of the rear wheels. Unique perch bars, constructed from armoured wood, projected forwards from the rear axle. All lighting was by acetylene and both summer (Clements) and winter (Dodson) bodies were available.

Morris

ONE-TON Six of these Kiddle-bodied 'chasers' were ordered in 1925. The three-speed 4cyl engine developed 14/28hp and offered 20 miles per gallon, but the demands made upon it meant that this was seldom achieved. The bench-type sponge-rubber seats frayed at the edges after only a few weeks use.

CDD 2/F Two so-called 'chassisless' 35-seat saloons by Beadle, purchased in 1949. For many years, they worked the service to Salisbury from the Winchester depot.

Shelvoke & Drewry

FREIGHTER One of these little vehicles was acquired at Swanage in 1927. The first 'full-fronted' vehicle operated by the company, it was fitted with a 12hp, 4cyl petrol engine and had solid-tyred wheels only 20in across. With the exception of an emergency foot-brake, all control was effected by tram-type handles each side of the driving seat. The left-hand handle regulated the transmission brake, forward speeds, reverse gear and the clutch, whilst the other steered the vehicle.

Star

50cwt One charabanc acquired from Trade Cars in 1920 and employed for several years at Southampton upon private hire work. It was powered by a 4cyl petrol engine and was fitted with a cape-cart hood, carried forward upon running supports.

Straker Squire

CO 5 Bournemouth & District's first four vehicles, these 4-ton charabancs were delivered in 1916. Bodywork was by Knight & Co and the petrol engines—with 4cyls cast in pairs—developed 45hp.

Thornycroft

J Type The first charabanc of this type was acquired from Trade Cars in 1920. Like the Maudslay from the same source, it was based upon an ex-Army Service Corps chassis. A further charabanc and a saloon omnibus were taken over with Enterprise at Gosport in 1924. Others followed, but were not operated. The 3½ ton 'J' was powered by a 4cyl petrol engine developing 30/40hp and was easily recognised by its large perforated wheel discs.

A 1 Long, A 2 Long An A 1 Long was acquired from Greyhound of Woolston in 1927. It was fitted with Wadham saloon bodywork and developed 25/40hp from its 4cyl petrol engine. A six-year-old A 2 Long with coach body by Ransome & Whitehead was acquired with Parma Violet Coaches in 1935.

GC/SC 6 'Lightning' A normal-control, canvas-roofed coach with Wadham bodywork, one example was delivered new for evaluation in Hants & Dorset's 1935 'Tourist, Southampton' fleet. It was powered by a 6cyl petrol engine.

A 6 One Wadham-bodied coach, then seven years old, was acquired from Rob Roy Coaches in 1935. 6cyl petrol unit fitted.

Vulcan

30cwt Two Paine & Frampton-bodied saloons were acquired

from Phipps of Netley in 1926. They were small one-man operated units powered by 4cyl petrol engines.

In addition, AEC 416, 417A, 426, 660; Crossley; Dennis 30cwt, G; Ford T; GMC T19; Guy B, BB, CPP; Reo 'Pullman'; Star 'Flyer' and other single deck types were acquired between the wars, but did not enter service. Six-seat Daimler and Humber saloon cars were included in the fleet list and operated by the Hire Car Department until World War II.

LIVERY AND INDICIA

Until 1930, all saloon buses were painted BAT dark green (the shade used by Maidstone & District until 1972) with broken-white roofs. Panels were lined in gold with ornate corners. The open toppers delivered during the twenties were the first to incorporate the new Tilling green (below the upper deck), but between 1930–72 Tilling green and cream became the standard company colours. Of the charabancs, the Silver Fleet were aluminium, the first two Leylands grey and all others BAT dark green. Coaches acquired from Royal Blue (dark blue, lined out in yellow) and Tourist (black and dark blue with cream band) retained their original liveries until the end of the 1936 season. Hants & Dorset's new coaches—including the Thornycroft 'Lightning' labelled 'Tourist'—had dark blue side-panels with ultramarine above (and chrome strips), but after 1936 this gave way to cream and Tilling green respectively—with BAT dark green wings. From 1951 all coaches, open toppers and convertible open toppers (and two Lodekkas used for four years on the Bournemouth–Southampton limited stop service) have been predominantly cream. By contrast, Shamrock & Rambler coaches within the fleet continued to operate in orange and cream livery.

Between 1936–46, coaches carried a buckled garter inherited from Elliott Brothers and inscribed HANTS & DORSET, ROYAL BLUE

Livery and Indicia: a restorer's guide. (*left*) The ornate corner motif (gold on BAT dark green) 1919–31, and (*right*) class letter style (gold and black on Tilling green) 1935–49. Both actual size

AND TOURIST; whilst until 1946, all service buses carried the shaded-gold fleetname in an arch-shaped format. This became the company's unofficial trade-mark, which survived into the seventies on the crews' cap badge. From 1946, the fleetname was applied in standard Tilling styles until, in October 1972, 5in 'National' style capitals in white were adopted, together with the 'double N' symbol. Now, after fifty-four years, the familiar 'green bus' has been repainted NBC red. What William Graham would have thought of that, I dread to think—even his yacht's burgee was green and gold!

Three separate numbering schemes have been used. The first, to which vehicle classification letters were added in 1931, utilised transfers thereafter and lasted until 1949.

VEHICLE CLASSIFICATION LETTERS ALLOCATED 1931–1949

A	Leyland GH7, TD3, 3c, 4 (4c later)
AD	Leyland TD 3 (oil-engined), TD2 (oil-engined, later M)
B	Leyland PLSC1, 3
BB	Leyland LT1
BG	Leyland LT5
BA	Leyland LT5a
C	Leyland PLSP2
D	Leyland PLA2
E	Leyland TD1
F	Leyland TS2, 3, 7, 8
G	Leyland TD2
H	Chevrolet X, LM, LQ
J	Lancia Pentaiota? AJS Pilot? Ford AA. AEC Regal
K	Guy OND. Dennis Ace
L	Leyland KP2, KPZ1, 2, 4
M	Leyland TD2 (revised model)
MD	Leyland TD2 (re-engined as oiler, later AD and M)
N	ADC 424. Daimler CF6
P	Gilford 168OT? Leyland TD4 with torque conv., (later A)
Q	AEC Q
R	Albion PH 49 (later S)
S	Sundries: various new, secondhand, re-classified buses
SC	Service cars, circa 1941
HC	Daimler, Humber hire cars of 6-seat capacity
TD	Bristol K5G, K6A, K6B
TS	Bristol L5G, L6A saloons
TC	Bristol L6G, L6A coaches
CD	Guy Arab 1
PD	Leyland PD1a

The second series—on metal plates, placed the vehicles in batches which, for the first time, separated 20-seaters, coaches, saloons and double-deckers. In 1971, this idea was incorporated in a new series which included the vehicles of Wilts & Dorset, with the numbers applied direct to the bodywork.

Three types of depot-allocation markers have been carried on the buses: small tablets attached above the near-side front window (1949–55), coloured number plates (1955–71) and coloured discs applied above the fleet number (1971 onwards).

Full fleet lists, reconstruction and disposal details have been published by the PSV Circle and the Omnibus Society, c/o 52 *Old Park Ridings, Grange Park, London N*21, *whose booklets PK*7 *and PK*8 *are recommended.*

POSTSCRIPT

Following the demise of the 'Wilts & Dorset' fleet name on 1 October 1972, the vehicles hereunder were 'added' to the Hants & Dorset list:

Bedford
- SB 13 Two coaches
- VAM 14 and 70 Five coaches and eight saloons
- YRQ Two coaches
- VAL 70 Thirteen coaches

Bristol
- KSW Eighteen low-bridge double-deckers
- LL Two dual purpose saloons (ex H & D, 1970)
- LS Twenty-seven saloons and seventeen dual purpose
- LD Thirty-seven 'Lodekka' double-deckers

Bristol (cont)
- MW Eight coaches (2 ex H & D, 1972) Fourteen converted to saloons, twelve saloons, seven dual purpose saloons
- FS Twenty-eight 'Lodekka' double-deckers
- FLF Twenty-six 'Lodekka' double-deckers
- RELL Twenty-six saloons
- LH Sixteen saloons

Leyland
- L1 'Leopard' one saloon

In January 1973, five PSU4/4R 'Leopard' coaches, of 1966 vintage and ex-North Western Road Car Co Ltd, joined the Hants & Dorset fleet.

APPENDICES

APPENDIX A

HANTS & DORSET OFFICERS

CHAIRMEN

Walter Flexman French Snr	1916–1926
Thomas Wolsey	1926–1931
George Cardwell	1931–1948
Raymond I. H. Longman	1948–1959
Thomas W. H. Gailey	1960–1965
David S. Deacon	1965–

DIRECTORS

		Representing
Walter Flexman French Snr	1916–1926	—
William Wells Graham	1916–1947	W. W. Graham & Co
Sidney Garcke	1916 Mar-May	BET
James McMeekin	1916–1924	—
James E. Spagnoletti	1916–1920	BET
Clarence S. Hilton	1919–1927	BAT
Thomas Wolsey	1920–1931	Thomas Tilling
Admiral Sir Edmund Warre Slade	1920–1928	BAT
Leopold M. Myers	1920–1923	BAT
George Wolsey	1924–1926	Thomas Tilling
Reginald M. Tilling	1926–1931	Thomas Tilling
Ralph G. Davidson	1930–1946	Southern Railway

Major-General Gilbert Szlumper	1930–1932	Southern Railway
George Cardwell	1931–1948	Thomas Tilling
Herbert A. Short	1932–1936	Southern Railway
Charles D. Stanley	1933–1942	BAT
John C. Chambers	1936–1939	Southern Railway
Charles W. G. Elliff	1939–1944	Southern Railway
Raymond I. H. Longman	1942–1959	Thomas Tilling
John C. Chambers	1944–1949	Southern Railway
Herbert A. Short	1946–1949	Southern Railway
Stanley Kennedy	1948–1949	Thomas Tilling

From 1 January 1949, appointments were made by the British Transport Commission and its successors

Albert E. Webster	1949 Feb-Oct	—
Frederick P. Arnold	1949–1955	Tillings Transport (BTC) Ltd
William H. F. Mepstead	1949–1960	British Railways (SR)
George H. Napthine	1949–1958	—
James W. Webb	1955–1956	British Railways (SR)
Charles P. Hopkins	1955–1956	British Railways (SR)
Maurice A. Holmes	1955–1960	—
Walter H. Scutt	1956–1959	British Railways (SR)
Douglas W. Morison	1958–1971	—
Arthur C. J. Payne	1959–1963	British Railways (SR)
Thomas W. H. Gailey	1960–1965	Tillings Transport (BTC) Ltd
Claude H. S. Pickett	1960–1964	Tillings Transport (BTC) Ltd
Stephen A. Fitch	1960 Apr 1–19	British Railways (SR)
Percy A. White	1960–1963	British Railways (SR)
Frederic P. B. Taylor	1963–1968	British Railways (SR)
George McKay	1964 Jan-Sept	Tilling Association Ltd
Ian R. Patey	1964–1965	Tilling Association Ltd
David S. Deacon	1965–	Tilling Association Ltd
Bernard Griffiths	1965–1966	Tilling Association Ltd
Thomas G. Pruett	1966–1968	Tilling Association Ltd
Stanley J. B. Skyrme	1968–1971	National Bus Company
George A. Weedon	1969–1970	British Rail (SR)
Ray S. Sandall	1970–1971	National Bus Company
Clifford A. Rose	1970–1971	British Rail (SR)
Ian R. Patey	1971–1972	National Bus Company
Llewellyn S. Edwards	1971–1972	British Rail (SR)
Peter C. Hunt	1972–	National Bus Company
Frank K. Pointon	1972–	National Bus Company

GENERAL MANAGERS

William Wells Graham	1916–1945
Albert E. Webster	1945–1949
George H. Napthine	1949–1958
Douglas W. Morison	1958–1971
Peter C. Hunt	1972–

SECRETARIES

Albert E. Webster	1916–1945
William J. George	1945
Ian R. Patey	1945–1947
Herbert Harding	1947–1965
Desmond G. Finley	1965–

TRAFFIC MANAGERS

A. S. Hansford*	1927 Jan-Sept
A. B. Wells	1927–1935
A. E. Webster†	1936–1945
D. W. Morison	1945–1958
S. Bartlett	1958–1967
J. M. Wadsworth	1967–

CHIEF ENGINEERS

Samuel E. Walton	1919–1927
William D. Moffatt	1927–1931
P. S. Pelling	1931–1935
H. N. Tuff	1935–1939
G. J. Brown	1939–1941
P. S. Pelling	1941–1949
G. R. E. Wallis	1949–1966
W. L. F. Henderson	1966–1968

* Traffic Superintendent. Prior to this appointment, Reginald Hewlett and E. G. Tilley performed administrative duties in the traffic sector.

† Also Secretary.

A. R. Smith*	1968–1969
A. Gurley	1969–

Between 1916 and 1919, William Graham performed the duties of engineer.

DEPOT MANAGERS 1945

H. W. Rollings	Bournemouth Tours
R. Perry	Poole
J. Hardy	Swanage
G. Vacher	Bere Regis
H. F. Harrison	Lymington
H. N. Crabb	Southampton
J. Jackson	Southampton Tours
E. G. Tilley	Winchester
W. Beney	Fareham
H. Barnes	Netley

DEPOT SUPERINTENDENTS 1972

G. W. Seymour	Bournemouth/Poole
C. S. Bennett	Swanage
B. A. Hoare	Lymington
I. J. Buchan	Southampton
S. A. Marsh	Winchester
H. D. Lever	Fareham
E. Warwick	Eastleigh (Depot Inspector)

DIVISIONAL MANAGERS 1973

G. W. Seymour	POOLE Bournemouth Lymington
I. J. Buchan	SOUTHAMPTON Winchester Eastleigh
J. P. Berkshire†	FAREHAM
J. G. Welling	BASINGSTOKE Andover
P. T. Fairweather	SALISBURY Pewsey Amesbury

* Acting Chief Engineer.

† Acting Divisional Manager, J. P. Berkshire is Assistant Traffic Manager (Comm) and Manager of Gosport & Fareham Omnibus Company.

APPENDIX B

FACTS & FIGURES

1: SHARE CAPITAL

1916–1920	£30,000	1930–1934	£350,000
1920–1925	£75,000	1934–1937	£550,000
1925–1929	£125,000	1937–1953	£700,000
1929–1930	£200,000	1953–	£1,450,000

2: FINANCIAL MILESTONES BEFORE NATIONALISATION

March 1916 Private company, largely underwritten by James MacMeekin, a 'gentleman of Ufford in Suffolk', formed with a nominal capital of £30,000. Director's qualifications: holding not less than 100 £1 shares of the company, in any class, in his own name. During 1919, Walter F. French disclosed that he had 'committed himself to a personal liability of about £90,000 in connection with the proposed motor services'.

February 1920 Capital increased to £75,000.

June 1924 £11,900 paid to Elliott Bros for 12 Daimler 'Charabuses', together with £7,500 in cash and £4,400 in fully paid £1 Ordinary shares, for the right to operate stage carriage services without competition from 'Royal Blue'.

July 1924 With the strengthening of the Tilling interest, H & D became a public company. This coincided with the parent (BAT) company's issue of £250,000 5½ per cent Debenture stock at £95 per cent. At the time, BET and Thomas Tilling held over 70 per cent of the British Automobile Traction Company share capital.

February 1925 Capital increased to £125,000.

March 1929 Capital increased to £200,000.

June 1930 Capital increased to £350,000, comprising 150,000 6½ per cent Preferential £1 shares and 200,000 Ordinary £1. (Tilling & BAT 33·3 per cent; Southern Railway 33·3 per cent).

June 1934 Cumulative Preference shares returning 4½ per cent at 29 shillings (£1.45); Ordinary shares yielding 4⅞ per cent at 52s 6d (£2.62½).

September 1934 £71,000 transferred from depreciation reserve to general reserve. Capital increased to £550,000 by the creation of 200,000 additional £1 shares. £120,000 of the general reserve capitalised and applied in distributing 120,000 Ordinary shares in the proportion of 3 new shares for every 5 Ordinary shares held.

October 1936 80,000 Ordinary £1 shares issued at par to ordinary shareholders in the proportion of one for every 4 held.

October 1937 Capital increased to £700,000 by the creation of 150,000 Ordinary £1 shares. £50,000 of the reserve capitalised and distributed as bonus to Ordinary shareholders, one new Ordinary share for every 8 held.

June 1938 Shareholders offered 100,000 new Ordinary £1 shares at par, 2 new shares for every 9 held.

September 1942 Tilling acquired the BAT interest and H & D became a subsidiary of the newly formed Tilling Motor Services Ltd.

December 1946 Capital reserve increased by an 'excess profits tax' post-war refund of £115,995.

March 1947 Earnings for the year permitted the distribution of a special 10 per cent tax-free bonus.

January 1948 The Southern Railway interest passed to the British Transport Commission.

March 1948 Another 10 per cent tax-free bonus for the year distributed.

September 1948 Tilling's shares sold to the BTC.

November 1948 Concern about the apparent lack of provision for the minority shareholders dropped H & D shares 10s (50p) to 100s (£5), despite a particularly buoyant period during the year.

February 1949 The BTC at last announced its intention to purchase the minority shareholdings, which promptly sent the market price of the ordinary shares plummeting a further 10s (50p) to £4 11s 6d (£4.57½).

April 1949 The BTC announced its terms of purchase, to be settled in BTC 3 per cent stock, valued at 101 per cent. Price per share: 6½ per cent cum. Preference, £1 9s 6d (£1.47½); £1 Ordinary, £4 11s 6d (£4.57½).

December 1949 Profit for the 9 months, 1 April–31 December was £160,513: dividend 6 per cent tax-free, with additional special bonus of 7½ per cent tax free.

3: PROFITS, ETC 1930–1948 (THE SOUTHERN RAILWAY ERA)

Year ending 31 *March*	*Net profit* £	*Dividend per cent*	*To reserve* £	*Carried forward* £
1930	34,252	12½	7,500	8,917
1931	37,423	,,	,,	10,020
1932	45,526	,,	,,	12,047
1933	37,583	,,	2,500	11,130
1934	39,977	,,	,,	12,356
1935	53,318	12½*	2,000	12,425
1936	55,059	12½	,,	14,234
1937	63,720	,,	,,	14,453
1938	64,039	,,	,,	19,993
1939	68,545	10	,,	20,038
1940	71,496	9¼	5,000	24,159
1941	66,269	9	,,	24,427
1942	65,165	,,	,,	23,591
1943	64,761	,,	,,	24,102
1944	65,899	,,	,,	25,750
1945	70,380	,,	,,	31,880
1946	92,705	,,	25,000	40,336
1947	137,618	19†	20,000	43,704
1948	254,709	,,†	100,000	84,163

4: SHARE CAPITAL SINCE NATIONALISATION 1950–1953

British Transport Commission	549,998 Ordinary
	150,000 Preference
Miles Beevor Esq	2 Ordinary‡

* After a share bonus of 60 per cent.

† Including a special bonus of 10 per cent tax-free.

‡ Transferred to Sidney Taylor Esq (1) and Reginald Wilson Esq (1), 6 November 1950.

1953–1962

(Share Capital raised to £1,450,000, December 1953)

British Transport Commission	1,449,998
Sidney Taylor Esq	1*
Reginald Wilson Esq	1*

1962–1968

Transport Holding Company	1,449,999
Transport Nominees Ltd	1

1969–

National Bus Company	1,449,999
THC Bus Nominees Ltd	1

* Transferred to Bri-Travel Nominees Ltd and Transport Nominees Ltd respectively, 10 March 1955.

APPENDIX C

ITEMS OF EXPENDITURE

(As listed in the Second Schedule of The Bournemouth Corporation Act, 1930 and taken into account in ascertaining the cost of carrying a passenger who both boarded and alighted, within the Bournemouth Corporation area, upon the same journey.)*

Fuel
Tyres
Lubricating oils
Drivers
Conductors
Inspection &c, tickets and punches
Cleaning and greasing
Car lighting (includes materials and bulbs)
Uniforms
Tolls and outside garage charges
Repairs to chassis
Repairs to bodies
Depot power light heat and water
Depot lorries and staff cars (running and upkeep)
Insurances
Publicity
Postage and other communications
Buildings (rents rates repairs &c)
Local depot staffs

* See Chapter Four, Bournemouth and General Progress: Boundary Changes.

Sundry expenses
Licences
Head office staff
Directoral administration
Depreciation of rolling stock and plant

APPENDIX D

1: CONDITIONS OF SERVICE FOR DRIVERS AND CONDUCTORS IN 1937—AN EXCERPT

Rates of Pay The standard weekly wage for drivers and conductors is as follows:

Omnibus drivers	£3 10s 0d (£3.50)
Conductors	£2 10s 0d (£2.50), rising annually at the rate of 1s 6d (7½p) per year to a maximum of £2 17s 6d (£2.87½)
Driver-conductors	By arrangement with the management
Coach drivers	£3 0s 0d

The company reserves the right to make special arrangements for pay for time spent on vehicles whilst on private hire or special trips, or other special duties.

Payment for Bank Holidays On Easter Monday, Whit Monday and August Bank Holiday, the company pays a bonus of 10s (50p) to each man working, provided the business done on these particular days proves successful. The company retains the right to withdraw this at any time. In addition, overtime is paid to all those members of the driving and conducting staff whose duties exceed 12 hours.

Privileges Drivers and conductors travelling to and from work may do so free of charge, providing they give up their seats to fare-paying passengers if the omnibus is loaded beyond its seating capacity. On stage carriage services, 6 free passes per annum will be granted to an employee, his wife and up to 2 children.

Annual Holidays Six days' holiday, with full pay, will be granted annually after one year's service. The holiday is to be taken at the period of the year assigned by the company.

Discipline Nothing in these conditions shall preclude the company from taking disciplinary action for dereliction of duty. In particular, the company may punish any employee by immediate dismissal on payment of one day's pay, or suspension from duty, for intoxication, sleeping on duty, disobedience to orders, negligence, misconduct, or being absent from duty without leave.

Welfare Society A staff welfare society is in existence, which drivers and conductors are invited to join. Information can be obtained from the depot managers.

2: CONDITIONS OF EMPLOYMENT IN 1937—AN EXCERPT

(5) One recognised day off in each 7 days. The term week consisting of 6 working days.

(6) The *average* hours worked per week being *approximately* 50–52.

(7) The company have no objection to men belonging to a trade union, but it must be definitely understood that they *do not recognise* Union conditions as to working hours or rates of pay.

(8) Overtime is paid for any additional journeys done that are not shown on the daily duty sheet. *EXCEPT WHEN ON THE FOLLOWING DUTIES: Sandbanks Route.* During the summer season a number of duties consist of *COUNTY GATES SPARE:* as the traffic on this route is according to the weather, etc, there are very slack periods during the day. Therefore *overtime is paid only in exceptional cases.*

(11) Conductors must report for duty *HALF HOUR* before being due out on service at the *COMMENCEMENT* of their day's duty. This is to enable them to properly check their ticket box before going on service. Any errors in their tickets, or the numbers on the waybill must be reported before going on duty.

Note. All starting times shown on the Duty Sheet refer to departure times on service from omnibus station or the terminus.

APPENDIX E

A SELECTION OF HANTS & DORSET TICKETS

A Standard H & D Bell Punch composite used until 1946. Carried in a wooden rack and held in place by spring clips, the following values were printed:

d		*s*	*d*		*s*	*d*	
1	Pale Khaki		10	Lilac	1	10	Pale Green
1½	Pale Orange		11	Pale Khaki	2	0	Straw Yellow
2	Pale Grey-Blue	1	0	Lilac	2	1	Bright Orange
3	Straw Yellow	1	1	Ecru	2	2	Grey-Blue
4	White	1	2	Pale Grey-Blue	2	3	Pale Pink
5	Yellow	1	3	Salmon	2	4	Straw Yellow
6	Pink	1	4	Pink	2	6	Salmon
7	Salmon	1	5	Lilac	2	8	Green
8	Pale Grey	1	6	Mustard	3	0	Cream
9	Pale Grey-Green	1	9	Cream	3	6	Pale Grey

B Bournemouth–Poole tramway replacement type. Nine tickets in series, rising in halfpenny lots 1d–5d. Ground colours same as corresponding value above. Overprinted red or green.

C BCT type for use within the Bournemouth Corporation Transport area (see Chapter Four). Modified forms used over a 40-year period (1930–70) ranged from 1d to 1s 5d.

D One of the numerous Bell Punch 'Through Tickets' available 1926–51 for exchange upon Southdown and Aldershot & District vehicles.

E The original form of 'Setright' return ticket (1946).
F A 'Setright' introduced following the closure of the Meon Valley Line. Fareham–Wickham (H & D), Wickham–Alton (Southdown).
G Continuous-roll 'Speed-Setright' tickets ousted the 'Setright'.

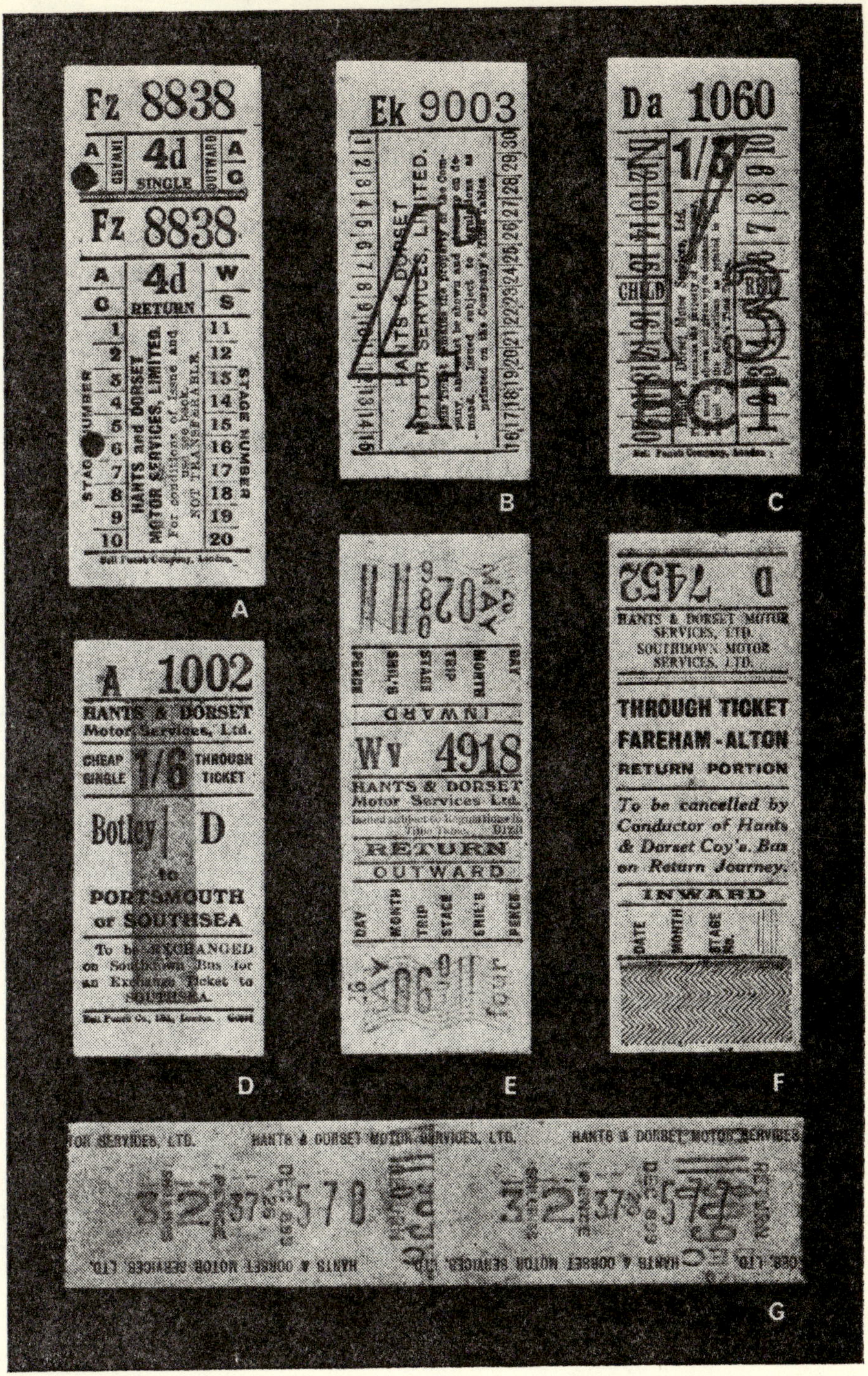
Fz 8838
4d SINGLE
Fz 8838
4d RETURN
HANTS and DORSET MOTOR SERVICES, LIMITED.
STAGE NUMBER
Ek 9003
HANTS & DORSET MOTOR SERVICES, LIMITED.
Da 1060
1/3
CHILD
A 1002
HANTS & DORSET Motor Services, Ltd.
CHEAP SINGLE 1/6 THROUGH TICKET
Botley D
to
PORTSMOUTH or SOUTHSEA
To be EXCHANGED on Southdown Bus for an Exchange Ticket to SOUTHSEA.
INWARD
Wv 4918
HANTS & DORSET Motor Services Ltd.
RETURN
OUTWARD
D 7452
HANTS & DORSET MOTOR SERVICES, LTD.
SOUTHDOWN MOTOR SERVICES, LTD.
THROUGH TICKET
FAREHAM - ALTON
RETURN PORTION
To be cancelled by Conductor of Hants & Dorset Coy's. Bus on Return Journey.
INWARD
HANTS & DORSET MOTOR SERVICES, LTD.
A
B
C
D
E
F
G

APPENDIX F

EARLY FARE LEVELS

IN THE accompanying graphs (which do NOT represent fares between INTERMEDIATE points), passengers travelling between the TERMINAL POINT and places shown BELOW the diagonal lines, paid more for their journey than—and, in effect, subsidised—those travelling to or from points ABOVE.

By comparison, one undertook an expensive journey along the comfortably populated Wickham to Southampton route at 2·4d (1p) per mile, and a cheap one from Blandford to Bournemouth at 1·5d (0·62p) per mile. Beyond Sturminster Marshall, tickets on the rural Shaftesbury run at that time cost an average 1·4d (0·58p) per mile to or from The Square. Least fortunate, in this respect, were passengers who travelled between County Gates and Sandbanks (not shown), and were charged 3d (1·2p) per mile. In recognition of this, reduced-rate residents' tickets in books of one dozen were available. Similar facilities were to be granted briefly, as services at both Swanage and Netley commenced. Elsewhere, the need to win passengers at the expense of the London & South Western Railway placed travel to the larger towns in the 'best buy' category.

In the early days, the only return ticket offered was the 1s 6d (7½p) from Poole to Sandbanks—1s (5p) single. It was not until 1924 that returns, issued at reduced rates, were introduced throughout the system—and until 15 March 1927, these were available for use upon the day of issue only. Children over three and under twelve years of age were charged at half the scheduled rates.

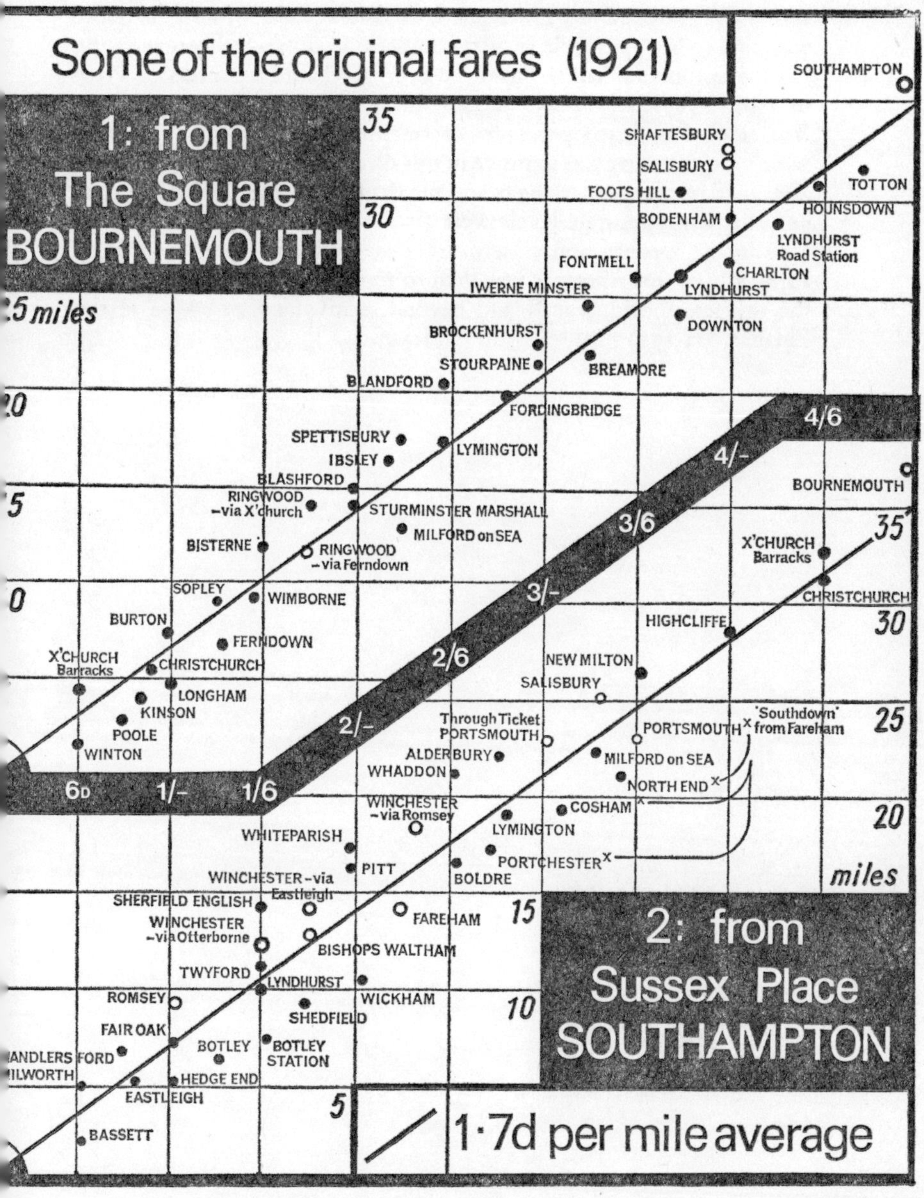

A comparative selection of Adult single fares on services in operation by December 1921

By 1927, virtually all the destinations shown had moved to the left across the graphs: from The Square, the average cost of a single ticket was 1·6d (0·66p) per mile, whilst competition on several routes in the Southampton area had reduced the average charge from Sussex Place to 1·4d (0·58p) per mile. (The short-lived Southampton to Lyndhurst fare at 0·3d (0·124p) per mile, represented the extravagant limit to which the company was to move in this direction.) Almost immediately afterward, the impact of the economic depression was duly recognised and the pence-per-mile levels were frozen marginally below 1·6d and 1·4d in the western and eastern areas respectively. Apart from local adjustments, this structure was then to remain unchanged throughout the thirties, World War II and beyond, until the after-effects of the Finance Act 1950 finally let slip the leash.

BIBLIOGRAPHY AND ACKNOWLEDGEMENTS

THIS BOOK is based upon a local-history study which I completed in 1957 whilst a student at Bournemouth College of Art: a thesis much influenced by the lectures of Frank E. Dodman, head of the Department of Art Education—and author of that well-known 'standard' *The Observer's Book of Ships*—and local-history scholar Robert Douch of the University of Southampton. Two years later, the department—clearly impressed—moved from its premises at the Lansdowne into the newly vacated headquarters of Hants & Dorset at 8 Bath Road.

Research for this volume recommenced in 1967 as a direct result of prompting by F. W. York, a writer well-known in omnibus circles. It was further encouraged and sustained by my wife's ex-boss, that much admired man-about-publishing, the late John Lloyd, AFC. Much of the content is concerned with personalities, establishment of routes, consolidation of territory and local background. Since vehicular detail has already appeared in a joint PSV Circle-Omnibus Society publication, comparatively brief references to company vehicles are summarised in Chapter Ten: to some specialists, the result will resemble the curate's egg, but for a volume of this size a considerable amount of data had to be stored against the future. Individual histories of some of the smaller operators mentioned do appear, however, in an occasional series entitled 'Hampshire Omnibus Operators' within *Hampshire*, the county magazine.

Background reading has included John Hibbs' *The History of British Bus Services*, to which readers wishing to learn more of the wider implications of national policy are directed; O. S. Nock's *London & South Western Railway* (1965); Bernard Knowles's

Southampton: the English Gateway (1951), which refreshed my memory of events within the town during World War II; B. C. Jones's *Crossing the Itchen* (1961) and Edwin Welch's *Southampton Maps from Elizabethan Times* (1964), both published by Southampton Corporation; articles in the following journals: *The Autocar*, *Bus & Coach*, *Commercial Motor*, *Hants & Dorset Motor Services Ltd Magazine*, *Leyland Journal* 1935–39, *Modern Transport*, *Motor Car Journal* and *Tramway & Railway World*; and the following newspapers: *Bournemouth Graphic* 1916–1920, *Hampshire Advertiser* 1900–1927, *Southern Evening Echo* and *Bournemouth Evening Echo*, *News & Mercury*, *Poole & Dorset Herald* and *Swanage Times & Directory*, and the *Financial Times*.

I have made considerable use of personal testimony and whereever possible checked statements of place, time and quantity against available records. Retrospectively, I must thank those who helped in 1957, notably Mr G. H. Napthine, then director and general manager: Mr H. W. Rollings, retired tours-manager: Wing Commander T. R. Cave-Browne-Cave of the University of Southampton: Messrs R. Perry and Charles Dunning. More recently I am indebted to Mr D. W. Morison, director and general manager of Hants & Dorset Motor Services Ltd until December 1971: Mrs L. M. Hawker, daughter of the founder: Miss Betty Webster, daughter of the second general manager. Among the many who have offered help and hospitality, but are not mentioned in the text are: Mrs W. E. Podesta, Mrs Colin Harfield, Ernest Bailey, Harry Bolton, Inspector Chapman of Woolston, W. L. Felmingham, John Henry, J. C. Holleyhead, W. A. Holmes, Eric Jones, Harold Leach, J. C. Ransom, L. E. Robbins, Fred Wheeler, Nigel Wheeler and J. T. Wilson. My task was also lightened by the friendly co-operation of: the city archivists of Southampton and Portsmouth; the town clerks of Bournemouth, Lymington and Poole; the controllers of licences for Bournemouth, Southampton, Hampshire and Dorset; the chief librarians of Bournemouth, Hampshire and Liverpool; the curator of Leicester Museum of Technology; the Spares & Service manager—and the picket line—at Transport Equipment (Thornycroft) Ltd; Vauxhall Motors Engineering Dept; Le Chef du Service Transports, P/Automobiles M. Berliet; Beadle's (Dartford) Ltd; Rutherford Photographic of Swanage; the publicity officer, Southdown Motor Services Ltd; and—in particular—the publicity manager and Photographic Department of the Brush Electrical Engineering Co Ltd and the public relations manager, the stationery, photographic and *Journal* staff of Leyland Motors Ltd, during my many visits to their premises. Philip Davies of Ferndown read several drafts as the book progressed and many of his suggestions are incorporated. Meanwhile, Andrew Waller and Robert Gray of Fareham loaned essential material—the latter for such a lengthy period, he must have believed he'd seen the last of it. For his contribution of the Foreword, many corrections and enthusiastic support throughout, I acknowledge my debt to Mr Harold J. Stevens, chief licensing officer of the company. The publisher and author are greatly indebted to Hants & Dorset Motor Services Ltd, especially for the provision of the map at the back of the book and for several of the blocks for line illustrations. Finally, a big thank-you to my wife Kate, who has proved an invaluable help at every stage.

ACKNOWLEDGEMENT OF PLATES

Leyland Motors Ltd: Jacket and pp 35b, 69b, 70b, 88b, 121a, 122a, 139r. Mrs Lory Hawker: pp 17a, 17r, 18a. William Cox: p 17. George Randall: pp 18b, 35a, 36a. Hants & Dorset Motor Services Ltd: pp 36, 69a, 70l, 87r, 122b, 174b, 191l, 191b. F. E. Wilkins: p 36b. Brush Transformers Ltd: pp 70a, 88a, 121b, 122, 140a, 173a. W. L. Felmingham: p 87a. J. C. Ransom: p 139l. Transport Equipment (Thornycroft) Ltd: p 139. *The News*, Portsmouth: p 173b. *Bournemouth Times*: p 174a. Philip Davies: pp 191a, 192b. Mrs Sybil White: p 192a. P 140b was photographed by the author.

Department of Education
Faculty of Art & Design
Liverpool Polytechnic

COLIN MORRIS

INDEX

References to illustrations are indicated by *italic* type